to keep you on
straight and nar

love from Sandra,
October 1983

WHAT I CANNOT
TELL MY MOTHER
IS NOT FIT
FOR ME TO KNOW

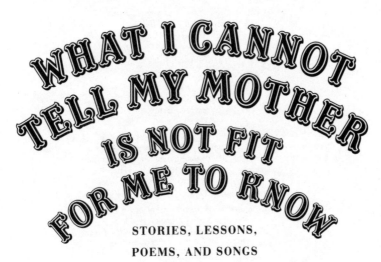

WHAT I CANNOT TELL MY MOTHER IS NOT FIT FOR ME TO KNOW

STORIES, LESSONS,
POEMS, AND SONGS
OUR GREAT-GREAT-GRANDMOTHERS AND
OUR GREAT-GREAT-GRANDFATHERS
HEARD, READ, AND SANG IN SCHOOL AND AT HOME

TAKEN MAINLY FROM SCHOOL TEXTBOOKS,
READERS, RECITERS, AND SONGBOOKS OF THE
NINETEENTH CENTURY

====

Chosen by Gwladys and Brian Rees-Williams

Oxford New York Toronto Melbourne
OXFORD UNIVERSITY PRESS
1981

Oxford University Press, Walton Street, Oxford OX2 6DP

London Glasgow New York Toronto
Delhi Bombay Calcutta Madras Karachi
Kuala Lumpur Singapore Hong Kong Tokyo
Nairobi Dar es Salaam Cape Town
Melbourne Auckland
and associate companies in
Beirut Berlin Ibadan Mexico City

Compilation © Gwladys and Brian Rees-Williams 1981

British Library Cataloguing in Publication Data
What I cannot tell my mother is not fit for me to know.
1. Children's literature, English
2. Moral development – Literary collections
I. Rees-Williams, Gwladys   II. Rees-Williams, Brian
820.8'0353   PZ5
ISBN 0-19-212223-1

Printed and bound in Great Britain
at The Pitman Press, Bath

For our grandsons
Seth and Luke and for
Pat Conroy

Many people have been good enough to remember their childhood for us. We thank in particular Mrs Caroline Rees, who is 96 and grew up in Talyllyn in Breconshire, Mrs Elsie Horsfield, 82, a girl in Wass in the North Riding of Yorkshire, and Mr Sidney Smith, 85, a Derby boy.

We are grateful for help to Allen Jones and Frances Walder of the College of Ripon and York St John, Geoffrey Summerfield and Jim Walvin of the University of York, Tom Young, HMI, Judith Chamberlain of OUP, and, especially, Jack Conroy of St Aelred's Primary School in York.

CONTENTS

ADVERTISEMENT

It was the object of the Editor, in forming the present Selection, to exclude all Poems which appeared to be, in any respect, unsuitable for young Persons, and, as far as it was practicable, not to admit any that had not a tendency to refine the taste, or to improve the heart.

Joseph Cottle, *Selection of Poems, designed chiefly for Schools and Young Persons*, c.1830.

I have no sweetmeats, cakes, or toys,
As gifts for little girls and boys;
But look in me, and you shall find
Both food and playthings for the mind.

Mrs Child, *The Girl's Own Book*, 1853

THE NEW BOOK

I am only a book, but I can tell you many things you would like to know.

Now I must ask you to take great care of me. You must not break my back, or I shall fall to pieces.

You must not smear me with black hands, or I shall not like any one to see me.

If you do not take care of me, and treat me well, I shall never be able to tell you all the nice tales I know.

Will you please to have a bag made to put me in when you do not want me?

You must not drop me into the pond on your way to school, for that would be the death of me, and I could then tell no more tales.

Ned had a new book just like me, but he broke its back, and it came to pieces. The leaves were lost, so he never knew what the book had to say.

But I think you will not serve me so, for you look so kind. And you will not be so rude as to talk while I tell my tales, so I will do my best to please you.

> Little girls and little boys,
> If you will not make a noise,
> But as quiet be as mice,
> I will tell you something nice.
>
> Learn to read and learn to spell,
> For you know I cannot tell
> All my tales, both short and long,
> Till you lend to me your tongue.

New Standard Story Books, *c.* 1880.

MONDAY

Laugh and Shout

The lark is up in the sky,
The meadows are bright with dew;
The lambs are playing, and why,
Dear children, should not you?
Out into the meadows, and leap and run,
And laugh and shout to the morning sun.

Matthias Barr, *Hours of Sunshine*, c. 1880.

Sleeping in the Sunshine

Sleeping in the sunshine,
Fie, fie, fie!
When the lark is soaring,
High, high, high!
While the birds are singing sweet,
And the flowerets at your feet
Look a smiling face to greet.
Fie, fie, fie!

Sleeping in the sunshine,
Fie, fie, fie!
While the bee goes humming
By, by, by!
Is there no small task for you –
Nought for little hands to do?
Shame to sleep the morning through.
Fie, fie, fie!

Matthias Barr, *The Child's Garland of Little
Poems*, c. 1870.

[3]

QUEEN VICTORIA'S REIGN

There have been many wonderful improvements made, and new things found out in Queen Victoria's reign – for instance, the penny postage. We think nothing *now* of writing a letter, and being able to send it anywhere – all over England, Scotland, and Ireland, for just *one penny*; but do you know that when Queen Victoria first became queen, people had to pay sixpence or eighteen-pence for every letter they sent by post, however small? So you can fancy people did not write very much in those days, only when they had something very important to say. People used to wait till a friend was going to the place, and get the friend to take the letter with them. Electric telegraphs, too, came into general use, and after a while were laid under the sea, so that messages could be sent between England and other countries.

The most difficult task, however, was to lay a wire between this country and America. It had to go thousands of miles along the bottom of the Atlantic Ocean. It was done, however, at last, after many trials. So now we can hear from America in one day, instead of waiting a whole fortnight for our news.

The streets of London were not always kept so safe and quiet by policemen as they are now. There used to be feeble, old watchmen, with lanterns, and boxes to stand in, who used to call out the passing hours all through the night, but the thieves and burglars did not fear them much. A great man, called Sir Robert Peel, in our queen's reign, thought of having proper policemen, both for day and night, to keep order in the London streets. And although Sir Robert Peel was much laughed at at the time, his plan has turned out a very good one.

In conclusion, there is one thing I especially wish you to remember, and that is, what a great and good Queen it has pleased God to place over us! I am sorry to say, in these days, you may often hear people wishing that there was no queen, and that England could be governed by the people only. But the people who wish this, surely forget that England has been a happier, richer, more powerful, and more Christian nation under our beloved Queen, than at any other time in England's history. Victoria is, indeed, a Christian queen, and *this*, more than all her great talents, has been the secret of England's present prosperity and greatness. Let us, then, unite in saying, from our hearts – God save the Queen!

Brenda, *Old England's Story in Little Words for Little Children*, 1884.

Hurrah for England!

Hurrah! hurrah for England!
Her woods and valleys green!
Hurrah for good old England!
Hurrah for England's queen!

(*Notes for teachers: Verse 1*. Let the children try and find out what they mean when they cry out – hurrah! What feeling do they all join in? A joyful thankful feeling. For what do they express themselves glad? For England. To what country do they belong? What reasons have they for being thankful for their country? Ask them to give you as many reasons as they can. It is a pleasant country; neither very hot, or very cold; supplies them with food; there are no slaves in it. They have schools to go to, they are taken care of, and no one allowed to hurt them; above all, God is worshipped in this land, and they have ministers to teach them, and Bibles to read. What is said in this verse that England has? What are woods? What are the uses of trees – when growing – when cut down? What makes the valleys green? What is the use of grass? Thank God for giving England

[5]

woods and valleys green. The children will now be able to say, why England may be called good; but why old? It has long been a country enjoying these blessings, preserved by the Almighty. Our fathers before us had them. Who is placed at the head of this country? A young Queen, and what are we to her? Her subjects. What is our duty? To love and honour her. That is God's command. Then shout for our Queen, as well as our country.)

> Good ships be on her waters,
> Firm friends upon her shores,
> Peace, peace within her borders,
> And plenty in her stores.

(*Verse 2*. What is all round our land? What is upon this water? What is the use of ships? They go to other countries, and bring things that are not produced in England. Let the children name some, to fix the idea in their minds – rice, coffee, tea, spices, sugar, etc. They protect us from our enemies in time of war. What has England on its shores? What is meant by firm friends? Tell me something you call firm. Which is firm, a tree, or a reed? Why do you consider a tree firm? It cannot easily be moved from its place, so a firm friend cannot be moved from being a friend. What two things is England enjoying? Peace and Plenty. What is it to be at peace? Here the children might have described to them something of the horrors of war experienced in other countries: houses burnt, women and children turned out of their homes or killed, crops destroyed; from this our happy country has been saved, and whilst war was going on in other countries, our ships preserved peace within our borders. And what does the earth every year produce for us? Supposing the crops were all to fail, what would there be then? A famine. Yes, and what then becomes of the people? They starve. But God year after year sends us a harvest, and has kept us from famine. It is a good land we live in. Well may we say, hurrah for England. That is, love our country and rejoice in it.)

> Right joyously we're singing,
> We're glad to have it known
> That we love the land we live in,
> And our queen upon her throne.

(*Verse 3*. How are you supposed to be singing these verses? What makes you joyful? What are you glad to make known? It would be a shame to you not to love your country and your Queen – let it be known that you love them, that others may join you, and the love may spread.)

> Then hurrah for merry England!
> And may we still be seen
> True to our own dear country,
> And loyal to our queen!

(*Verse 4*. What then will you shout out? What is England called? What desire are you taught to express? How can you be true to your country? First, in your heart or feelings. Think often and gratefully of the advantages you enjoy. Love your country and be thankful to God for placing you in such a country. Secondly, in your words, speak well of her, never murmur against her, or abuse her, and pray for her. Thirdly, in your actions – obey her laws, respect all in authority, be honest and industrious. And how can you be loyal to your Queen? Love her, pray for her; never speak ill of her, never listen to those who would try to make you discontented with her, but ever be ready to say from your heart, God save the Queen.)

Model Lessons for Infant School Teachers and Nursery Governesses, by the Author of 'Lessons on Objects', 1842.

The Hay-Field

Make hay while the sun is shining,
In the morning of life make hay;
A child like you but little can do,
Yet work a little he may,
Yet work a little he may.

He who cannot load a waggon
Can a little go-cart fill;
The stack will grow
And its size show
You have work'd with a heart and will.

What small drops make the ocean!
What grains of sand the shore!
Let it be confess'd
You have done your best, –
A giant can do no more.

The Illustrated Book of Songs for Children,
c. 1863.

Naughty Johnnie

Johnnie had the measles,
So he lay in bed;
And he didn't listen
To a word his mother said.
He wouldn't take the medicine,
He tossed away the spoon;
I think that Johnnie cannot
Get better very soon.

The tortoise went to see him,
It never spoke a word;
I think that it was frightened
By all the noise it heard.
The cat looked quite astonished,
The kitten ran away.
Oh, what a very naughty boy
Was Johnnie on that day!

The Prize for Boys and Girls, 1889.

LESSONS ON DOMESTIC ECONOMY

LESSON XXII · MAKING A FIRE

1. There are two methods of kindling a fire: one is to light it at the top; the other, to light it at the bottom. Both have their merits and their advocates; but whether the one is to be chosen rather than the other depends upon the purpose for which the fire is wanted.

2. When the fire is required merely to warm the room, then a slow uniform rate of burning is the best, and may be secured by lighting the fire at the top. When this method is pursued, the bottom of the grate should be covered with a sheet or iron, or tin plate, or even a piece of thick brown paper will do. This plate should be so fitted as to exclude the draught, and force the air to enter at the front. On the plate should be laid fresh coal until the grate is nearly full, and on the coal the wood arranged in order. The wood should then be covered with some good cinders. When the wood is kindled, the fire thus produced will pass slowly downwards through the coal. As the fire burns downwards the smoke from the freshly ignited coal will have to pass through the fire and be consumed. Such a fire should never be poked; in fact it does not require it; to poke it is to spoil it.

3. When the fire is required to burn up rapidly, it should be lighted on the second plan, from the bottom, which is, in fact, the usual way. Very few girls, or even young women, lay a fire properly, and, as a consequence, they waste a great deal of fuel. Attention to the following rules for laying a fire will prevent this waste.

First. – First rake out all the ashes; this done, put some cinders in the bottom of the grate. Do this with care, and so arrange them that they reach up to the first bar of the grate, except in the middle of the front, where there should be a small space to hold some crumpled paper. Next place some sticks of wood a small distance apart, and so arranged that one end of the stick rests on the first bar of the grate.

Second. – Do not fill up the whole grate, but leave a space on each side; in these place some small lumps of coal. Now place another row of sticks across the first row, taking care that they do not touch each other. Again place a few pieces of coal at the sides. Add another row of sticks on the top of the last, but placed in the same direction as the first row, taking care that there are spaces left between each stick. Now put some coal all round the top, but leave a space in the middle without any coal. Also put some lumps between the bars. Place some crumpled paper in the space left for it between the lowest bar and the bottom of the grate. Light the paper, and place the kettle over the hole left in the middle, but be careful not to let the kettle rest on the coals. This can be managed by putting three or four lumps of coal a little above the rest at the top, and on these place the kettle.

4. Directly the paper is lit the wood will take fire, and the flame will pass up the hole left in the middle and play upon the bottom of the kettle, and so the water will have some heat the very instant that the fire is kindled, and receive it where it is most useful.

5. To lay a fire in this manner requires care, and occupies some time. It is, however, time well spent, and the result will repay the care bestowed. If well laid, a fair-sized kettle of water can be boiled in a very short time, and this without the fire requiring to be poked, thus leading to a great saving of fuel, an important item at the present day.

6. When the fire needs poking, stir it at the bottom; do not break up the lumps at the top, for in doing this a considerable quantity of coal will fall out, and may be wasted. When the fire requires fresh coal, put it on with a shovel; do not throw it on from the scuttle. If the fire is not wanted to burn up quickly, as, for instance, between dinner and tea, press it well together, and put on some small coal; the very smallest will do. Wet these before you put them on, and press them well when you put them on. After a time these will cake together, and when the fire is wanted give it a gentle stir from the bottom, and there will be a bright cheerful fire.

A small fire constantly fed is not so economical as a fair-sized one made up in the manner described above.

QUESTIONS ON LESSON XXII

1. Describe the two methods of kindling a fire.
2. When is the one to be preferred to the other?
3. Describe the method of lighting a fire at the top.
4. State how you would lay a fire which is to be lit at the bottom.
5. What are the advantages of this mode? How does it save fuel and time?
6. How should you poke a fire?
7. Why is not a small fire fed so economical as a large one made up at once?

Joseph Hassell, *Lessons in Domestic Economy for Elder Girls, c. 1890.*

Song of the Farmer's Boy

This is the way my father sows
His oats, as through his field he goes;
And when the grain springs from the ground
He folds his arms, and gazing round,
Says, –
'Soft rain fall, and bright sun shine,
And make my oat crop fine!'

This is the way my father reaps
His oats, and when they lie in heaps,
In yellow heaps, upon the ground,
He folds his arms, and gazing round,
Says, –
'Rain keep off, and bright sun shine,
And make my oat crop fine!'

This is the way my father binds
His oats in sheaves, and when he finds
No more remaining on the ground,
He folds his arms, and gazing round,
Says, –
'Thanks to rain and bright sunshine,
My oat crop has been fine!'

This is the way my father's oats
Are made to lose their husky coats;
And when the flail rings on the ground
He folds his arms, and gazing round,
Says, –
'Come what will, come rain or shine,
My crop is housed in time.'

Songs and Lyrics for Little Lips, c. 1880.

THE KID AND THE WOLF

A Kid that had strayed away from the rest of the flock was caught by a Wolf.

'I know you will kill me,' said the Kid; 'but before you do so, please play me a tune so that I may have one more dance before I die. I am very fond of dancing.'

'Very well,' said the Wolf, as he took up a flute that was lying near. 'I will play for you, because I should like to see you dance before I eat you; but be quick, for I am very hungry.'

The Wolf played and the Kid danced. The Dogs were watching the flock some distance away, and, hearing the noise, they wondered what was the matter. When they reached the spot they saw the Wolf playing and the Kid dancing.

They at once sprang upon the Wolf, and were about to kill him, when he said –

'Why did I listen to the Kid? My business is to kill kids and eat them, not to play for them.'

To this the Kid, now out of harm's way, answered –

'You did not play very well either.'

MORAL: Those who do not mind their business will sooner or later come to grief.

My Book of Fables, c. 1895.

THE MILKMAID

A milkmaid was one day tripping gaily over the fields with a fine jar of milk upon her head. She was going to sell the milk at a neighbouring village, and pleased herself with thinking how much she would be able to get for it.

'Let me see,' she said to herself, 'milk sells now for fourpence a quart: I shall certainly be able to get two shillings for all I have in this pail.

'Then with that I will buy some butter; and if I take it to market, I may be able to sell it for half-a-crown. That will buy me two dozen of fresh eggs, which I will set under our best hen. When they are hatched, there will be four-and-twenty fine young chickens.

'In a couple of months they will be ready to kill, and I shall get half-a-crown a couple for them. Let me think: how much will that make in all?' But as she began to reckon her gains, she quite forgot the jar which she carried on her head. Down it fell, and every drop of milk was lost.

She had to go home without her butter, without her chickens, and without even her pail of milk. Her mother gave her a hearty scolding, and would often afterwards say to her, 'Daughter, remember the pail of milk. Do not reckon your chickens before they are hatched.'

The Granville Series Reading Book, Fourth Series, *c.* 1880.

The Hobby Horse

Hop, hop, hop!
Go and never stop;
Where 'tis smooth, and where 'tis stony,
Trudge along, my little pony,
Go, and never stop.
Hop, hop, hop!

Hey, hey, hey!
Go along, I say,
Don't you kick, and don't you stumble,
Don't you tire, and don't you grumble,
Go along, I say.
Hey, hey, hey!

Jump, jump, jump!
Don't you hit that stump.
Never will I cease to ride you,
Till I farther yet have tried you;
Don't you hit that stump.
Jump, jump, jump!

The Grade Lesson Book, First
Standard, *c.* 1870.

The Hidden Treasure

A farmer once, about to die,
Called on his children to come nigh.

'I leave,' he said, 'a small estate,
But means enough to make it great;
For, know, a treasure it contains,
If you to search will take the pains.'

He died. The sons dug all the ground,
But there no hidden treasure found;
Yet so productive was the soil,
The crop soon overpaid their toil.

'This was the hoard our sire foretold!'
Said one, when they their corn had sold.

Work, then, my boys, with hand and mind;
And labour you will fruitful find.

Royal Readers, No. III, Third Series, 1880.

DO WHAT YOU CAN

There was once a farmer who had a large field of corn; he ploughed it and planted the corn, and harrowed and weeded it with great care, and on his field he depended for the chief support of his family. But after he had worked hard, he saw the corn begin to wither and droop for rain, and he began to have fears for his crop. He felt very sad, and went over every day to look at his corn, and see if there was any hope of rain.

[15]

One day as he stood looking at the sky, and almost in despair, two little raindrops up in the clouds over his head saw him, and one said to the other: 'Look at that farmer; I feel sorry for him, he has taken so much pains with his field of corn, and now it is drying up; I wish I could do him some good.'

'Yes,' said the other, 'but you are only a little raindrop; what can you do? You can't even wet one hillock.'

'Well,' said the first, 'to be sure I can't do much, but I can cheer the farmer a little at any rate, and I am resolved to do my best; I'll try. I'll go to the field to show my good will, if I can do no more; and so here I go.'

The first raindrop had no sooner started for the field than the second one said:

'Well, if you are going, I believe I will go, too; here I come.' And down went the raindrops – one came pat on the farmer's nose, and one fell on a stalk of corn. 'Dear me,' said the farmer, putting his finger to his nose, 'what's that? A raindrop! where did that come from? I do believe we shall have a shower.'

By this time a great many raindrops had come together to hear what their companions were talking about, and when they saw them going to cheer the farmer and water the corn, one said: 'If you are going on such a good errand, I'll go, too,' and down he came. 'And I,' said another, 'and I,' and so on, till a whole shower came, and the corn was watered, and it grew and ripened – all because the first little raindrop determined *to do what it could.*

Emilie Poulsson, In the Child's World, 1893.

HOW TO KEEP YOUR ROOM

A look into the bedroom of a boy or girl will give one an idea of what kind of a man or woman he or she will probably become. A boy who keeps his clothing hung up neatly, or a girl whose room is always tidy, will be apt to make a successful man or woman. A boy who throws down his cap or book anywhere will never keep his accounts in shape, will do things in a slovenly, careless way, and will not be long wanted in any position. A girl who does not make her bed until after dinner – and she should always do it herself rather than have a servant do it – and throws her dress or bonnet down on a chair, will make a poor wife in nine cases out of ten. It is such little things that reveal the character, and such little acts of carelessness that grow into strong habits.

The Children's Friend, March 1899.

To Teach the H

Has Harry hopped over the hedge, Ann?
Has Albert felt hot in the air?
Ah, hand him to Hodge at the edge, Ann,
And hang up his hat on his hair.

Has Edith hired hampers for all, Ann?
Has Alice ate half of the eels?
Has Oswald his horse in the hall, Ann,
To hold up his elegant heels?

Has Ernest had all Harold had, Ann?
His egg and his herring to eat?
Is anything here he can add, Ann,
And have it at animal heat?

Jennett Humphreys, *Laugh and Learn*, 1890.

HEALTH OF HOUSES – I

1. There are five essential points for securing the health of houses, viz.: – pure air, pure water, good drainage, cleanliness, and light. Without these no house can be healthy. And it will be unhealthy just in proportion as they do not exist.

2. To have PURE AIR, your house must be so built that the outer air may find its way with ease to every corner of its interior. House builders do not always consider this. Their object in building a house is to obtain the largest interest for their money, not to save doctors' bills to the tenants.

3. But if tenants ever become so wise as to refuse to occupy unhealthily built houses, builders will speedily be brought to their senses. Bad houses do for the healthy what bad hospitals do for the sick. Once insure that the air in a house is stagnant, and sickness is certain to follow.

4. No one thinks how much disease might be prevented, even in the country, by simply taking care to provide the cottages with fresh air. Sometimes one more pane of glass made to open and shut, and put into the wall where it is wanted, will make a cottage sweet which always has been musty.

5. Sometimes a skylight made to open will make an attic wholesome which never was habitable before. Every careful woman will spread out the bedding daily to the light and the air.

6. No window is safe, as has often been said, which does not open at the top, or in which at least a pane in the upper row of the upper sash does not open. In small crowded rooms the foul air is all above the chimney-breast, and is therefore quite ready to be breathed by the people in the room.

7. This air requires to be let off; and the simplest way of doing so is one of these, namely –

    (i) An Arnott's ventilator in the chimney, close to the ceiling.
    (ii) An air-brick in the wall at the ceiling.
    (iii) A pane of perforated glass in a passage or a stair window.

8. The large old fireplace, under which three or four people could sit – still to be seen in cottages in the south of England, and in old manor houses – was an immense benefit to the air of the room. Pity it has disappeared in all new buildings! But never stop up your chimney. Of whatever size it is, it is a good ventilator. And during almost every night of the year, pull down your window an inch at the top. Remember, at the top.

9. PURE WATER is more general in houses than it used to be, thanks to the exertions of a few. Within the last few years a large part of London was in the daily habit of using water polluted by the drainage of its sewers and water-closets.

10. This has happily been remedied. But in many parts of the country well-water of a very impure kind is used for domestic purposes. When epidemic disease shows itself, persons using such water are almost sure to suffer.

11. Never use water that is not perfectly colourless and without taste or smell. Never keep water in an open tub or pail in a sitting room or a bedroom. Water absorbs foul air, and becomes foul and unwholesome in consequence; and it damps the air in the room, making it also unwholesome.

12. Many people have no idea of what good DRAINAGE consists. They think that a sewer in the street, with a pipe leading to it from the house, is good drainage. All the while the sewer may be nothing but a place from which sickness and ill-health are being poured into the house.

13. No house with an untrapped, unventilated drain-pipe, communicating immediately with an unventilated sewer, whether it be from water-closet, sink, or gully-grate, can ever be healthy. An untrapped sink may at any time spread fevers and other diseases among the inmates of a palace even.

14. Country cottages suffer from bad drainage quite as much as, if not more than, town houses. Their floors are sometimes on the level of the ground, instead of being a foot or more above it, as they ought to be, with the air playing freely below the boards.

15. More frequently, however, the floors are not boarded, but are merely made of earth or of porous brick, which absorbs a large

quantity of the moisture, and keeps damp cold air about the feet. Perhaps most frequently of all, the floor has been worn away several inches below the level of the ground, and of course after every wet day it is wet and sloppy.

16. But this is not the worst: sometimes a dunghill or a pigsty is kept so close to the door, that the foul water from it, after rain, may be seen flowing into the house.

17. Have you ever observed that there are certain groups of houses over which the fog settles sooner than over others? The fog is nature's way of showing that the houses and their neighbourhood are saturated with moisture from the neglects above specified.

18. These fogs also point out where the fever or the cholera will come. To remedy this state of things, the ground requires to be drained or trenched, the earth cut away, the floors raised above the level of the ground, and dunghills and pigsties removed as far as possible from the houses.

19. One of the most common causes of disease in towns is having cess-pools, ash-pits, or middensteads close to the houses. There are great and rich cities and towns which justly pride themselves on their drainage, their water-supply, their paving and surface cleansing, and which yet have more death in their dwellings than many towns where no such works have been carried out.

20. There is no way of putting a stop to this terrible loss of life except by putting an end to these cess-pools and ash-pits, and by bringing in drainage, as has been done in many of the very worst districts of London.

21. Among the more common causes of ill-health in cottages is overcrowding. There is, perhaps, only a single room for a whole family, and not more than 150 or 200 cubic feet for every inmate. Nothing can make such a room healthy. Ventilation would improve it, but still it would be unhealthy.

22. The only way to meet this overcrowded state of cottages is by adding rooms, or by building more cottages on a better model.

The ordinary oblong sink is an abomination. That great surface of stone, which is always left wet, is always exhaling hurtful vapours. I have known whole houses and hospitals smell of the sink.

23. I have met just as strong a stream of sewer air coming up the back staircase of a grand London house from the sink, as I have met at Scutari; and I have seen the rooms in that house all ventilated by the open doors, and the passages all unventilated by the closed windows, in order, apparently, that as much of the sewer air as possible might be conducted into and retained in the bedrooms. It is wonderful!

The Granville Series Reading Book, Fourth Standard, *c.* 1880.

I Must Not Tease My Mother

I must not tease my mother, for she is very kind,
And everything she tells me I must directly mind;
For when I was a baby, and could not speak or walk,
She lull'd me in her bosom, and taught me how to talk.

I must not tease my mother, and when she likes to read,
Or when she has the headache, I'll silent be indeed;
In play I'll not be noisy, or trifling troubles tell,
But sitting down beside her, I'll try to make her well.

I must not tease my mother, she loves me all the day,
She tells of God and heaven, and teaches me to pray;
How much I'll strive to please her, she every hour shall see,
For should I lose my mother, what would become of me?

John Curwen (ed.), *Songs and Tunes for Education*, 1861.

BE NOT CRUEL

There is one thing which some children do, which is a great sin; and it will be well if you can be kept from doing as they do.

They are fond of hurting God's creatures, such as flies and birds. Some rob poor birds of their eggs. The poor things cannot talk, but they can feel when they are used in this cruel way.

A cruel boy will be a cruel man. A great king, who killed flies for sport when he was a boy, killed men and women for sport when he grew to be a man. And he was killed himself at last.

If you ask, May we not kill any thing that would hurt us? I say, Yes, you may, if you do it quickly, and not in sport; but your parents had better do it than you.

All creatures are for some use; and some which we think evil, are for some good. There are many, too, like the busy bee, that would not hurt us if we did not hurt them.

A good boy will be fond of his rabbit, or his bird, and will fetch food for it, and will be pleased when he sees it jump or fly about as if it were happy.

These creatures know when we use them well, and when we use them ill. The dog and the horse always know a good master, and are fond of him. Even the ass knoweth his owner, if he be kind to him.

Besides, as these creatures are not able to speak, we ought to be all the more kind to them. If it be cruel to tease or hurt a dumb boy or girl, it is also cruel to tease or hurt a dumb creature.

Again, the same great and good God who made you, made them too. He made them for our use, and if we abuse them, He will be angry with us.

> Sweet it is to see a child,
> Always tender, always kind;
> Ever ready to perform
> Acts of mercy to a worm.

The New Class Books for Sabbath Schools: Second Reading Lessons, *c.* 1875.

LESSONS IN READING – THREE LETTERS

THE TOY

No, no! no toy for Ben, nor cup, nor cat, nor bow, nor bat. He is a bad boy. He got a fly, and ran a pin in it. And yet one day how he did cry as Joe ran a pin in his arm!

O Ben, it is a sin for you to vex the fly, as it is a sin for Joe to try to vex you.

It may vex any fly to put a pin to it or to hit at it, as it may vex any boy to do so to him, or to box or rap him.

And O! let us not do sin, or act in any bad way. For the eye of God is on us.

He can see all we do.

He it is who is a joy to all who are in woe, and no foe to any one; to you, or to me; to the ant, or the bee; the fly, hog, cow, fox, owl, jay, tit, cat, rat, dog, ape.

For as he is the God of you, and of me, and of all men; so is he the God of all we can see.

So let us not do ill, or act or do in any way so as to vex him. Hap as hap may to us, yet God is a God to all. So be it.

Crusts in Soak for Chickens to Peck, or, The Little One's Reading Book, by Pa, 1838.

THE BOY AND THE NETTLE

Two boys were playing in the fields, when one of them struck the ball into a bed of nettles. The other Boy ran to get it, and in doing so he was badly stung.

Crying with pain he went to his Mother, and told her what had happened.

'You should have been more careful,' said she, 'and no harm would have come to you.'

'But, Mother,' he replied, 'I hardly touched the Nettle.'

'That is just it,' she said. 'If you touch a Nettle gently it will sting you, but if you grasp it firmly it will not hurt you.'

MORAL: Boldly face a difficulty or a danger if you wish to overcome it.

My Book of Fables, c. 1895.

CONSCIENCE

A little boy called Jem Roberts, having been set to weed in a gentleman's garden, saw some very fine peaches on a tree which grew on a wall, and was strongly tempted to pluck one. 'If it tastes half as nice as it looks,' he thought, 'how very nice it must be!' He stood for an instant gazing on the tree, while his mother's words, 'Touch nothing that does not belong to you,' and the words of the Bible, 'Thou shalt not steal,' came into his mind. He withdrew his eyes from the tempting object, and went on with his work. He forgot the fruit, and was soon pleased to find he had nearly reached the end of the bed he had been told to clear. So he raked his weeds in a heap, and went to put them in his barrow, which stood near the peach tree. Again the glowing fruit met his eye, more tempting than ever, for he was hot and thirsty. He stood still – his heart beat. He looked up and down, and all around. There was no one but himself in the garden. He forgot his mother's words and his Bible too.

'They can never miss one out of so many,' he said to himself – he made a step. 'Only one' – he was now within reach of the prize: he darted forth his hand to seize it, when at the very moment, a sparrow in a tree near, calling to his mate, seemed to his startled ear to cry, 'Jem! Jem!' He sprang back upon the walk, his hand fell to his side, his whole frame shook; and as soon as he could, he fled from the spot. Then he began to reason with himself:

'If a sparrow could frighten me thus, I may be sure that what I was going to do was very wicked.'

And now he worked harder than ever; nor did he once again trust himself to gaze on the fruit. The sparrows chirped again as he was leaving the garden, but they did not frighten him this time.

'You may cry Jem! Jem!' said he, looking up at the tree in which ten or a dozen of them were perched, 'as often as you like; I don't care for you now; but this I will say – I will never forget how good a friend one of you has been to me, and I will rob none of your nests again.'

The Grade Lesson Book, First Standard, *c.* 1870.

The Nurse's Song

Sleep my child, my darling child, my lovely child, sleep:
The sun sleepeth upon the green fields,
The moon sleepeth upon the blue waves.
Sleep my child, my darling child, my lovely child, sleep.

The morning sleepeth upon a bed of roses,
The evening sleepeth on the tops of the dark hills.
Sleep my child, my darling child, my lovely child, sleep.

The winds sleep in the hollow of the rocks,
The stars sleep upon a pillow of clouds.
Sleep my child, my darling child, my lovely child, sleep.

The mist sleepeth in the bosom of the valley,
And the broad lake under the shadow of the trees.
Sleep my child, my darling child, my lovely child, sleep.

The flower sleeps while the night dew falls,
And the wild birds sleep upon the mountains.
Sleep my child, my darling child, my lovely child, sleep.

The burning tear sleepeth upon the cheek of sorrow,
But thy sleep is not the sleep of tears.
Sleep my child, my darling child, my lovely child, sleep.

Sleep in quiet, sleep in joy, my darling,
May thy sleep never be the sleep of sorrow.
Sleep my child, my darling child, my lovely child, sleep.

A Little Book for Little Readers, by the Editor of the 'Parting Gift', 1837.

Evening Hymn

At the close of every day,
Lord, to Thee I kneel and pray,
Look upon Thy little child;
Look in love and mercy mild.
Oh, forgive, and wash away
All my naughtiness this day;
And, both when I sleep and wake,
Bless me for my Saviour's sake.

Hymns and Rhymes for Children, c. 1875.

TUESDAY

A Child's Morning Prayer

I thank thee, Lord, for quiet rest,
And for thy care of me:
Oh! let me through this day be blest,
And kept from harm by thee.

Oh, let me love thee! kind thou art
To children such as I;
Give me a gentle, holy heart,
Be thou my Friend on high.

Help me to please my parents dear,
And do whate'er they tell;
Bless all my friends, both far and near,
And keep them safe and well.

A Poetry Book for Schools, 1879.

Shout and Bawl

Shout and bawl,
And run and fall,
And up and at it again.
If you must run,
And have the fun,
You must also have the pain.
It's only by knowing the sweet from the sour
That you'll gather wisdom, and strength, and power.

Matthias Barr, *Hours of Sunshine, c.* 1880.

QUITE A MAN

'I think I shall soon be quite a man,' said Tom to a girl whom he knew well, as she sat by the gate of her home.

'Well,' said she, 'some boys think they are men, but they act as boys for all that. If you were a man, Tom, you would not throw plum stones at me. You would not tease my dog. You would not put your foot out to make me fall down. You would not laugh when you see rude boys do things which you know are wrong.

'You may be a *big* boy, and you may be an *old* boy, but I shall not think you a man till you act like a man. No true man would do a mean thing. A true man is brave and just. He will do what is right, and fear not. Think of *that*, Tom.'

'Yes,' said Tom, 'I will. What you say is quite true. I must try to be a good boy, that I may grow up to be a good man.'

Royal Readers, No. I, First Series, 1895.

The Squirrel

We caught a young squirrel, right here in our wood.
He tries to get out; and he will, if he's good –
If only he's good, if only he's good.
He tries to get out; and he will, if he's good.

The wind, it was shaking the nuts from the trees;
One dropped on his nose and made him to sneeze.
He picked them all up – yes, he did – with his toes,
And laid them in order in beautiful rows.

Then he knelt in the grass and he made him a nest,
And ate up his nuts and sat down for a rest.
And he dropt off to sleep on that warm afternoon,
And he slept on and on till the middle of June.

The cuckoos were calling, one fine day in June,
And they woke him with trying to teach him the tune.
Cuckoo!
Cuckoo!

The Joyous Book of Singing Games, collected by John Hornby, *c.* 1890.

NO COWARD

'A fight! a fight! let's go and see the fight!' said John to Harry as they came out of school one fine summer's morning.

'No,' said Harry firmly; 'my mother expects me to go straight home when I leave school. Besides, I do not like fighting, and do not think it is right.'

'Ah! you're a coward,' said John, with a sneer; 'I shall go.' So John went to see the fight, and told all his schoolmates what Harry had said.

When they came out of school next day all the boys called after Harry, 'Coward! coward, go home, coward!' Harry took no notice of this, for he knew that he was no coward, and that he had done only what was right.

A few days after, a number of the boys went to bathe in the river, and as the season was fine and warm, they splashed about for a long time. All at once they heard a loud cry as of some one in distress. Soon they saw that it was John, who had got out of his depth, and was drowning.

Now surely you would think that all the boys who called Harry 'coward' rushed in to help him! No; they were all afraid, and only ran away to look for some one else to do it. Alas! he would have been drowned long before they came back, had not Harry come by just at the time, and seen what was the matter. He threw off his coat and shoes, and was in the middle of the stream in a very few moments, and, just as poor John was sinking for the last time, he got hold of him. The drowning boy clung to Harry with dying despair, and almost pulled him under water with himself. But Harry tried with all his might, and at last got poor John to the bank. Then he fainted. All thought John was quite dead, and they knew that Harry had had a narrow escape. Some people had now come up, who took the two boys to the nearest house. A doctor was sent for, and, under proper treatment, they were both well enough to go home before night.

Do you think John and his schoolmates called Harry a coward after this?

The Grade Lesson Book, First Standard, *c.* 1870.

Whistle Away

Whistle away, my merry boy,
With happy face, and heart of joy;
If it will help you to be strong,
Whistle a tune when things go wrong.
And whistling lightens it for you,
If e'er your task is hard to do.
Whether it be sowing the seeds,
Hoeing the corn, or pulling weeds,
Gathering fruit, or raking hay,
Or driving cows – whistle away.

Whistle a tune, if you can't sing,
And that should seem the next best thing
That you can do; perhaps 'twill cheer
The hearts of those who chance to hear.
Better to whistle than to pout,
And scold, and fret, no one can doubt;
So keep a merry heart, my lad,
And thus make other people glad;
Do you all the good you can each day,
And as you toil, whistle away.

Chambers's Recitations for the Children, selected by
R. C. H. Morison, *c.* 1900.

Make Your Mark

In the quarries should you toil,
Make your mark;
Do you delve upon the soil,
Make your mark;
In whatever path you go,
In whatever place you stand –
Moving swift or moving slow –
With a firm and honest hand,
Make your mark.

Life is fleeting as a shade –
Make your mark;
Marks of SOME kind MUST be made –
Make your mark;
Make it while the arm is strong,
In the golden hours of youth;
Never, never make it wrong;
Make it with the stamp of TRUTH –
Make your mark.

The Boys' Own Magazine, 1858.

LESSONS ON DOMESTIC ECONOMY

LESSON XXV · ALCOHOLIC, OR STRONG DRINKS

All alcoholic drinks are intoxicating, and, therefore, ought not to be taken by young people. The alcoholic drinks consumed in this country are ardent spirits, wines and beer.

1. *Ardent Spirits.* – (i) By ardent spirits is meant gin, whisky, hollands, rum and brandy. These consist almost entirely of spirit, colouring matter, and water. The proportion of spirit varies very

much. The least amount which may be put in is fixed by law, and that which contains the proper amount is called proof; if it contains more, it is said to be over proof; if less, under proof.

(ii) The proper place for these compounds is as a medicine, administered by the advice of a medical man. When thus administered, they may at times be beneficial, acting as stimulants to the stomach, and causing a quicker circulation of blood. Their constant use, however, is very objectionable.

(iii) The habit of dram-taking is one of England's misfortunes, and is the cause of much poverty and crime. Young women should never accustom themselves to drink ardent spirits, and should never keep company with those persons who do.

2. *Wines.* – Pure wines contain substances which may be of service in the nutrition of the body, and if administered by medical advice may be very useful in certain weak states of health. Wines are either strong or light. All the elements which are supposed to give any value to wines, except the alcohol, which has been added, are found equally in what are called light wines; and hence ordinary claret is quite as useful to the system under ordinary conditions of health, as port or sherry; at the same time claret is less intoxicating. Still, it cannot be too deeply impressed upon the young that the use of wines is, under ordinary circumstances, quite unnecessary, and should not be indulged in.

3. *Beer.* – (i) Both porter and ale contain substances which may be regarded as food – as sugar, gluten, and various salts. Beer is known as new and old, strong or weak. New beer may be either strong or weak. Old beer is always strong in alcohol. Some old ales contain as much as 25 per cent of alcohol, a quantity quite sufficient to produce intoxication. Some of the mild ales contain as much as 10 to 15 per cent of alcohol. Ale, as it advances in age, loses its gluten and sugar, and gains in alcohol and acid.

(ii) Bitter beers are thin and clear, and are perhaps more medicinal than any kinds, as the increased quantity of hops used gives them a tonic effect which is very beneficial.

(iii) London porter is of a very dark colour, owing to the fact that what is called black malt – that is, malt very highly baked – is used. When pure it contains about three-quarters of an ounce of alcohol in

KEPT IN

the pint. It contains more sugar and less hops than the pale ales. It is very seldom sold in its pure state. Its strength is reduced by water, and then treacle, liquorice, salt, and various narcotics are added to make up for the loss of alcohol.

According to the opinion of the highest medical authorities in this country, the use of alcoholic drinks is not only wholly unnecessary for the maintenance of health, but they are injurious in most cases, even when taken in quantities usually considered moderate. The experience of those Life Assurance Companies who insure the lives of abstainers in a separate section from those who are not abstainers, demonstrates that abstainers have a greater longevity than those who do not abstain.

HOW MUCH TO DRINK

As to the amount of drink of any sort taken during the day, it should be regulated according to the wants of the body, and not by mere habit. Too much liquid taken into the stomach interferes with the action of the digestive fluids; and this results in loss of health. The writer knew an artisan who, always feeling unwell, sought the advice of a medical man. The doctor questioned him as to the quantity of drink he took daily, and this was his account:- 'Well, doctor, I generally have a pint of coffee at half past six o'clock, and another pint at eight – breakfast time.' 'Well – what more?' 'Why, at eleven I have a pint of porter, and another at dinner.' 'Yes: any more?' 'Why yes; I generally have about a pint of porter at four o'clock, and then I don't have any more until about six o'clock, when I have about a pint of tea.' 'Yes, and what in the evening?' 'Why, you see, I have a glass or two of ale in the evening – not more than a pint I should say, and then I have about a pint at supper; that's all.' Thus he had eight pints daily, in addition to the water contained in his food, which was considerable. The doctor told him to diminish the quantity taken at meal-times, and leave off drinking between them, and at the end of a month to see him again. He did so; and very soon found himself improved in health, and much better off in pocket.

PRACTICAL RULES

1. Avoid over-drinking at meals: large draughts of water or beer chill and disorder the stomach, rendering it unfit to perform the functions of digestion.

2. Thirst is not quenched by imbibing large quantities of liquid at one time.

3. Do not accustom yourself to drink for mere drinking's sake.

4. Do not accept every invitation to drink. Have courage enough to say 'No,' when pressed to drink.

5. Never form friendships with those persons who are given to drinking habits.

QUESTIONS ON LESSON XXV

1. What is included in the term 'strong drinks'?

2. Why should ardent spirits not be drunk?

3. What bad habit should all young persons avoid?

4. What is wine? Under what conditions should it be used?

5. What are the different kinds of beer drunk?

6. What is the opinion of the highest medical authorities with reference to the use of alcoholic drinks?

7. What rules should be regarded as to drink?

Joseph Hassell, *Lessons in Domestic Economy for Elder Girls*, c. 1890.

Suppose!

Suppose, my little lady,
Your doll should break her head;
Could you make it whole, by crying
Till your eyes and nose are red?
And wouldn't it be pleasanter
To treat it as a joke,
And say you're glad 'twas Dolly's,
And not your head, was broke?

Suppose you're dressed for walking,
And the rain comes pouring down;
Will it clear off any sooner,
Because you scold and frown?
And wouldn't it be nicer
For you to smile than pout,
And so make sunshine in the house,
When there is none without?

Suppose your task, my little man,
Is very hard to get;
Will it make it any easier
For you to sit and fret?
And wouldn't it be wiser,
Than waiting like a dunce,
To go to work in earnest,
And learn the thing, at once?

Suppose that some boys have a horse
And some a coach and pair;
Will it tire you less, while walking,
To say, 'It isn't fair'?
And wouldn't it be nobler,
To keep your temper sweet,
And in your heart be thankful
You can walk upon your feet?

And suppose the world don't please you,
Nor the way some people do;
Do you think the whole creation
Will be altered, just for you?
And isn't it, my boy or girl,
The wisest, bravest plan,
Whatever comes or doesn't come,
To do the best you can?

Chambers's Expressive Readers, Book II, 1892.

THE FOX AND THE LION

A Fox was walking through a wood one day, when he heard a terrible noise. He was so afraid, that he ran and hid himself in a cave where a wolf lived.

'Can you tell me,' said he to the wolf, 'who made that terrible noise?'

'That was the roar of a Lion,' said the wolf.

'Dear me, how terrible! I thought I should die of fright,' said the Fox.

A few days after this the Fox was in the wood again, when the Lion began to roar.

'I wish,' said he, 'that the Lion would not make such a noise. It disturbs me more than I can tell.'

The Fox had now got used to the sound, and did not fear it as he had done at first. The third time he heard the Lion roar he said –

'I will go and look for that Lion. I wonder what is the matter with him, that he makes so much noise.'

Off ran the Fox to look for the Lion, and soon found him. When the Lion saw the Fox coming, he gave a louder roar than before, which shook the forest; but the Fox was not the least afraid. Going up to the Lion, he boldly said –

'Look here! What are you making all that noise about? It's horrible. I wish you would be quiet, and let us all live in peace.'

The Lion did not think that any beast would dare to speak to him

[42]

in that way; and he was so much surprised, that he walked off without saying a word.

MORAL: Dangers and difficulties often grow less the more we look at them.

My Book of Fables, c. 1895.

THE ECHO

'Hop, hop, hop!' shouted little Henry, as he was playing in a field near a wood.

'Hop, hop, hop!' came an echo in reply.

'Who is there?' asked Henry in surprise; for he had never heard an echo before.

'Who is there?' replied the echo.

'Foolish fellow!' cried Henry, at the top of his voice.

'Foolish fellow!' came the reply from the wood.

At this Henry became very angry, and called out many ugly names. The voice from the wood sent back every word.

Now, when Henry could not see who was speaking from the wood, he ran home and told his father that a boy hidden in the wood had called him bad names!

'Ah, Henry!' said his father, 'you have heard nothing but the echo of your own words. The bad names came first from your own lips. Had you used kind and gentle words, you would have had kind and gentle words in return. Kind words bring back kind echoes.'

The New Royal Readers, No. II, *c. 1885.*

YOU WILL NEVER BE SORRY

For using gentle words.
For doing your level best.
For being kind to the poor.
For looking before leaping.
For hearing before judging.
For thinking before speaking.
For harbouring clean thoughts.
For standing by your principles.
For asking pardon when in error.
For being generous to an enemy.
For showing courtesy to your seniors.
For giving an unfortunate person a lift.
For doing what you can to make others happy.
For refusing to take an unfair advantage of a school-fellow.

The Children's Friend, March 1899.

THE PIG IN THE GARDEN

Look! look! the pig is in the garden, and he has done a great deal of mischief. He has rooted up some of the potatoes that were planted only a week ago, and he has eaten six young cabbages.

Thomas has taken a whip, and with the help of the dog he will drive the pig out of the garden. How did the pig get into it? I will tell you.

James went into the garden to do some work. He forgot to shut the gate. The pig came along, and saw it wide open; and so he walked in.

There he found the cabbages, and many other nice things; so he at once set to work and ate them up.

The pig was not to blame, for he did not know that he ought not to go into the garden. But James was to blame, for he left the gate open. He was careless when he forgot to shut the gate.

How often children go to school without having learned their lessons! When the teacher asks them why they have not learned them, their reply is, 'Please, sir, I forgot.'

Would it not be correct to say rather, 'Please, sir, I did not take the trouble to remember?'

Some children think there is no harm in forgetting to do their duty. But that is a great mistake. If they do not remember their own business, no one will remember it for them.

If you forget a thing once, you may forget it again and again. In this way you may get into the habit of forgetting – a very bad habit, and a habit very hard to get rid of.

Royal Readers, No. II, Third Series, 1879.

The Little Maid

There was a little maid
Who wore a great big bonnet,
And she had a little frock
With a great big bow upon it.
She took a little walk
Along the great big road,
And on a little stone
She saw a great big toad.
It gave one little croak
And took a great big leap,
Which made the little maid
Give just one great big squeak.

New Standard Story Books, *c.* 1880.

[45]

Wicked Willie

Willie was a wicked boy,
Snubbed his poor old mother;
Willie was a dreadful boy,
Quarrelled with his brother;
Willie was a spiteful boy,
Often pinched his sister;
Once he gave her such a blow
Raised a great big blister!

Willie was a sulky boy,
Sadly plagued his cousins;
Often broke folks' window panes,
Throwing stones by dozens;
Often worried little girls,
Bullied smaller boys;
Often broke their biggest dolls,
Jumped upon their toys.

If he smelt a smoking tart,
Willie longed to steal it;
If he saw a pulpy peach,
Willie tried to peel it;
Could he reach a new plum-cake,
Greedy Willie picked it;
If he spied a pot of jam,
Dirty Willie licked it.

If he saw a poor old dog,
Wicked Willie whacked it;
If it had a spot of white,
Silly Willie blacked it;
If he saw a sleeping cat,
Horrid Willie kicked it;
If he caught a pretty moth,
Cruel Willie pricked it.

If his pony would not trot,
Angry Willie thrashed it;
If he saw a clinging snail,
Thoughtless Willie smashed it;
If he found a sparrow's nest,
Unkind Willie hid it.
All the mischief ever done,
Folks knew Willie did it.

No one liked that horrid boy,
Can you wonder at it?
None who saw his ugly head
Ever tried to pat it.
No one took him for a ride –
Folks too gladly skipped him;
No one gave him bats or balls,
No one ever tipped him.

No one taught him how to skate,
Or to play at cricket;
No one helped him if he stuck
In a prickly thicket.
Oh no! for the boys all said
Willie loved to tease them,
And that if he had the chance,
Willie would not please them.

And they shunned him every one,
And they would not know him;
And their games and picture-books
They would never show him;
And their tops they would not spin,
If they saw him near them;
And they treated him with scorn,
Till he learnt to fear them.

Tuesday

They all left him to himself,
And he was so lonely;
But of course it was his fault,
Willie's own fault only.
If a boy's a wicked boy,
Shy of him folks fight then;
If it makes him dull and sad,
Why, it serves him right then!

Pretty Poems for Young People, c. 1900.

THE TRUANT

As little Harry was sent to school one fine morning in June, he said to himself, 'What a shame to send a poor little chap like me to sit in a close school-room and learn lessons all day, when it is so much nicer out of doors! I'll not go to school this morning, but play about instead.'

So he walked up and down the lane, and then into the meadow, and back to the lane again; but soon got tired of being alone. So he spoke to a little boy whom he saw: 'Will you come and play with me?' 'No, I cannot,' said the boy, 'for I am going on an errand.'

Then he spoke to a horse that he saw feeding on the long grass under the hedge. 'Come and play with me,' said he, catching hold of the horse's mane. 'No, no,' answered the horse, shaking his head, and nearly throwing poor Harry into a ditch, 'I have no time for play; I must make haste and get my breakfast, for my master will want me soon to fetch coals from the railway.'

Then Harry called to a bee that was buzzing about and dipping first into this flower and then into that. 'Will you come and play with me?' 'Play!' said the bee, with his head inside a fox-glove, 'what does that mean?' 'Why, doing all one can to amuse one's-self without working,' said the boy. 'Oh, no! never did such a thing in my life,' answered the bee; 'for if I do not make honey in the summer, what shall I do in the winter? buzz, buzz, buzz.'

'Do come and play with me,' said Harry to a sparrow he saw hopping about the road. 'Couldn't think of such a thing,' said the sparrow with a worm she had just caught, wriggling about in her mouth, 'I am getting food for my children at home, bless their little hearts! but if I were to go and play the morning away with you, I should perhaps find them all dead when I got back to my nest.'

'Why, they all seem to be at work but myself,' said Harry. 'I don't feel so happy as I thought I should, and being away from school is not so nice either. I'll go to school now.' So he ran off, and I have heard that Harry never again felt a wish to play the truant.

The Grade Lesson Book, First Standard, *c.* 1870.

A Little Woman

When I'm grown up, said little Sue,
I'll tell you what I mean to do:

I'll gather fruit, and shell the peas,
And save the honey of my bees;

I'll make the tarts, and boil the jam,
And poach the eggs, and fry the ham.

I'll chop the herbs, and make the broth,
And clean the knives, and lay the cloth;

I'll dust the parlour and the hall,
And talk to all the folks that call.

Cosy Corner Pictures: stories and rhymes for little folk, c. 1902.

HEALTH OF HOUSES – II

1. Without CLEANLINESS within and without your house, ventilation is, to a great extent, useless. In certain foul districts poor people used to object to open their windows and doors because of the foul smells that came in. Rich people like to have their stables and dunghill near their houses. But does it ever occur to them that, in cases of this kind, it would be safer to keep the windows shut than open?

2. You cannot have the air of the house pure with dungheaps under the windows. These are common everywhere. And yet people are surprised that their children, brought up in 'country air', suffer from children's diseases. If they studied Nature's laws in the matter of children's health, they would not be so surprised.

3. There are other ways of having filth inside a house besides having dirt in heaps. Old papered walls of years' standing, dirty carpets, dirty ceilings, uncleaned furniture, – these pollute the air just as much as if there were a dungheap in the basement.

4. People are so little used to consider how to make a home healthy, that they either never think of it at all, and take every disease as a matter of course; or, if they ever entertain the idea of preserving the health of their household as a duty, they are very apt to commit all kinds of 'negligences and ignorances' in performing it.

5. Even in the poorest houses, washing the walls and the ceilings with quick-lime wash twice a year would prevent more disease than you know of.

6. A dark house is always an unhealthy house, always an ill-aired house, always a dirty house. Want of LIGHT stops growth, and promotes scrofula, rickets, and other diseases among children. People lose their health in a dark house; and if they get ill, they cannot get well again in it.

7. Three out of many 'negligences and ignorances', in managing the health of houses generally, I shall here mention as specimens:- (i) That the mistress of any house, large or small, does not think it necessary to visit every hole and corner of it every day. (ii) That it is not considered necessary to air, to sun, and to clean every room, whether inhabited or not. (iii) That the window is considered enough to air a room.

8. Have you never observed that a room without a fireplace is always close? If you have a fireplace, do not stop up the throat of the chimney. If your chimney be foul, sweep it; but don't expect that you can ever air a room with only one opening – don't suppose that to shut up a room is the way to keep it clean.

9. I have known cases of sickness quite as severe in private houses as in any of the worst towns, and from the same cause – namely, foul air. What was the cause of sickness being in that nice private house? It was, that the sewer air from an ill-placed sink was conducted into all the rooms, by carefully opening all the doors and closing all the passage windows.

10. It was that the chamber crockery was never properly rinsed, or was rinsed with dirty water. It was that the beds were never properly shaken, aired, picked to pieces, or changed. It was that the carpets and curtains were always musty, and that the furniture was always dusty.

11. It was that the wall-paper was soaked with dirt, that the floors were never cleaned, and that the empty rooms were never sunned or aired. It was that the cupboards were always full of foul air. It was that the windows were always fast shut up at night. It was that no window was ever regularly opened, even in the day, or that the right window was never opened at all.

12. Now, all this is not fancy, but fact. In the house referred to there have been in one summer six cases of serious illness – all the immediate products of foul air. When, in temperate climates, a house is more unhealthy in summer than in winter, it is a certain sign of something wrong. Yet nobody learns the lesson.

The Granville Series Reading Book, Fourth Standard, c. 1880.

Cradle Song

Night now draws her curtain round,
Hushed is every noisy sound,
Not a cricket's chirp is heard,
Not a song of little bird,
Yet my little baby lies
Wide awake with round blue eyes.

Every thing has gone to rest,
Birdie in the soft warm nest,
Little lambs within the fold,
Safe from fox or wolf so bold,
Yet my little lambkin lies
Wide awake with wondering eyes.

Mrs Charles Heaton, *Routledge's
Album for Children*, 1871.

MY COT

As I lie in my cot, I can see the sky.
I like to look at it, and see the stars come out, in the dark blue.
Soon the moon will come up, so bright and large.
I like that best of all, for it makes my room all light.
Good night, pretty moon; I must go to sleep now.

Longmans' 'Ship' Literary Readers: the Second Primer, 1895.

WEDNESDAY

Morning Hymn

Father, Thou hast heard my prayer,
And I own Thy tender care;
For, by Thee in safety kept,
I have laid me down and slept.
Teach me now my heart to raise
In a morning hymn of praise;
And for Jesus' sake, I pray,
Bless and keep me through the day.

Hymns and Rhymes for Children, c. 1875.

TOLERATION

'I shall have to change my quarters if this sort of thing goes on,' said Toby, a fat pug, as he stretched himself on the barn-door step and blinked his eyes at the sun; 'what with the cows, and the pigs, and the poultry, I can't get a wink of sleep for the noise!'

'Oh, it's quite unbearable,' said a tabby cat who was sitting inside the doorway watching a hole where a mouse had disappeared a few minutes before. 'One has no peace of one's life, and I should have had that mouse just now, if it hadn't been for Rover giving that sharp bark that frightened him straight into his hole.'

'And the night is as bad as the day,' said Toby; 'for when the fowls have stopped their cackling and gone to roost, and everything else is quiet, you and your friends raise the neighbourhood with the row you make. You'll forgive my saying so, but I think it's worse than all the rest put together.'

'Indeed,' said the cat with her back up, 'under these circumstances you'll excuse my mentioning a remark I overheard this morning, that if something wasn't done to stop you from walking round and round the house a dozen times a day with your nose in the air, barking at nobody, you would find yourself some day with a noose round your neck; every one is agreed that it is a most intolerable nuisance and must be put a stop to.'

'Ah!' said Toby thoughtfully, as he laid his nose between his paws and watched the cat disappearing up a ladder into the loft; 'there may be some truth in what she says, and I suppose I brought it upon myself; but it never struck me before how differently one listens to a noise one makes one's self, and a noise made by other people.'

Eleanor B. Prosser, Fables for You, c. 1895.

Gentleman John

You've only a fustian coat, my lad,
You sleep upon straw, maybe;
When my lord goes by it makes you sad,
You want to be rich as he.
You hate to be called a son of the soil,
You'd like to be gentleman born,
Never to want, and never to toil,
And never go tattered or torn.
But broadcloth or fustian, what you've got on,
Never will make you a gentleman, John.

'Tis not the honest brown dirt, my lad,
Makes a man's hand unclean;
'Tis what he does that is base and bad,
'Tis what is cruel and mean.
Don't be ashamed of your coat or your toil,
Each has his work to do;
See that you faithfully stick to the soil,
And you'll be a gentleman too.
'Tis what you have *in* you, not what you have *on*,
That ever will make you a gentleman, John.

Little Recitations for Little Readers, selected by
R. C. H. Morison, 1898.

BROTHERS AND SISTERS

Now there is another thing for little folks to regard, and that is, that they should live in peace with their own brothers and sisters. For this is right and good.

For you have all the same father and mother, who provide you with food and clothing. You live in the same house, and perhaps sleep in the same bed; and with each other you eat and drink, and talk and pray.

Should you not then try to be good friends? And if you do not agree ought you not to forgive each other, and so be good friends again?

Avoid giving offence; then you will live in peace. So never take the book or play-thing off your brother or sister without their leave.

And never do to them as you would not like them to do to you. This is called the golden rule, and if you go by it, you will not hurt or tease each other, or fall out about trifling things.

For it is not a pleasant thing to be always falling out. It is much better to live in peace and love. Your parents will be happy to see you do so, and the great God will be pleased too.

And mind one thing: brothers and sisters love you more than any other boys or girls in the world, and were you to die they would weep very much. And this shows that they love you.

Learn then to live, not like the dogs and cats which snap and snarl and bite, but like the pretty doves and harmless lambs which agree with each other.

Beside, the Word of God says, 'Little children, love one another'; and the Word of God is ever good and true.

And then, if you live in love on earth, one with another, and love the blessed Saviour who died for our sins, you will meet with each other again in a better world than this.

And will not that be a good thing, for fathers and mothers, and brothers and sisters, to meet in heaven at last?

The New Class Books for Sabbath Schools: Second Reading Lessons, *c.* 1875.

Pence Table

TO BE LEARNED BY HEART

Twelve pence will one shilling make,
Enough some pretty toy to buy;
Sixteen pence are one and four-pence,
That will get a kite to fly.

Eighteen pence are one and six-pence,
Which is only two-pence more;
Twenty pence are one and eight-pence,
The price of Lucy's battledore.

Twenty-four pence make two shillings,
This I paid to go by rail;
Thirty-two pence, two and eight-pence,
That will buy four quarts of ale.

Thirty-six pence are three shillings,
Paid for dinners on the road;
Forty pence are three and four-pence,
That I at the station owed.

Forty-eight pence make four shillings,
They for bat and ball will pay;
Fifty-four pence, four and six-pence,
Thus I hope to earn some day.

Sixty pence five shillings make,
This is also called a crown;
Sixty-six pence, five and six-pence,
Saved to buy mamma a gown.

Seventy-two pence are six shillings,
Paid some London sights to see;
Eighty pence are six and eight-pence,
Making up a lawyer's fee.

Eighty-four pence, seven shillings,
This was paid for my new hat;
Ninety pence, just seven and six-pence,
Bought a goose, large, plump, and fat.

One hundred pence are eight and four-pence,
What a many things 'twill buy;
To make nine shillings, take eight more pence,
This you'll prove, if you but try.

One hundred, next, and twenty pence,
Will just unto ten shillings come;
One hundred, then, and thirty-two,
Eleven shillings is that sum.

In pence, one hundred, forty-four,
Twelve bright shillings you may see;
When I have got so great a store,
We'll have a treat, – both you and me.

Thus every time we add twelve pence,
One shilling more we gain;
Two hundred, then, and forty-pence,
Will to a pound attain.

And thus, my dears, if you attend,
You'll by this table know,
How pennies up to shillings mount
And then to pounds may grow.

Then let me hope you'll take good care
How you despise a penny;
For PENNIES come, in time, to POUNDS,
And ONE POUND oft makes MANY.

T. Morell, *Papa and Mamma's Easy Lessons in Arithmetic, c.* 1845.

THE PEACHES

One day a man who had been to market brought home five peaches. His four sons met him on his return, and he said, 'There, lads, I have brought a peach for each of you, and one for your mother.' They took the fruit, with many thanks.

At night, before they went to bed, the father said, 'Well, boys, I should like to know how you liked the peaches, and what you did with them. Now let one speak at a time, and each shall give me his account.'

The eldest said, 'I ate mine, and found it very full of juice. I have put by the stone till the spring, when I mean to plant it, and hope to see a young peach-tree grow up.'

'That's right,' said his father, 'never waste anything. It is right to think of the future.'

The youngest then said, 'I ate mine, and threw the stone away, and mother gave me half hers. It was so nice; it melted in my mouth.' 'Well,' said his father, 'you are a little boy, and know no better; but you should not have been so hasty in eating the peach, and throwing away the stone.'

The next boy said, 'I picked up his stone and ate the kernel, and sold my peach for as much as will buy me three peaches next market day.'

The father looked grave, and said, 'It is right to think of the future, but you have acted in a way likely to lead to selfish habits. Avoid, my boy, a greedy, grasping spirit.'

The other boy said, 'I gave mine to lame George, who is ill with fever, and his friends are too poor to buy nice things for him. The doctor said ripe fruit would do him good.'

The other three felt this one had made the best use of his peach, and the tears of joy in his mother's eyes were better to him than a sack full of fruit.

The Grade Lesson Book, First Standard, *c.* 1870.

Stay in Your Seat

Have you forgotten the road to your mouth,
Whether it lies in the north or the south?
Feeding your eyes and your nose with your dinner
Won't make you fatter, but very much thinner.
Besides, who would kiss such a queer-looking boy?
Mamma won't behold you with feelings of joy.
Next time you are given your dinner to eat,
Please do it more cleanly, and stay in your seat.

Matthias Barr, *Hours of Sunshine*, c. 1880.

LESSONS ON DOMESTIC ECONOMY

LESSON XXIX · CLEANLINESS
CLEANLINESS OF PERSON

1. Apart from the pleasure of being clean, there is a necessity for it, arising from the nature and work of the skin. If the skin is examined with a magnifying glass, it will be found full of small openings – pores, as they are called. These openings are the ends of very minute tubes, about 1/300 of an inch in diameter and ¼ of an inch long. These are imbedded in the dermis, and communicate with the sweat glands. The number of pores vary in different parts of the body. They are fewest in the back of the neck, and most numerous on the palms of the hands and the soles of the feet: here they are about three thousand on a square inch. It is calculated that in the entire skin of an average-sized adult there are from two millions to two millions and a half of these tubes. Taking the number at two millions, and the length at ¼ inch, there will be nearly eight miles of tubes, and these may be called the drain-pipes of the house.

At the bottom of the dermis are a number of fat-cells, which supply the skin with an oily substance which keeps it supple.

[64]

2. The skin is not only a covering to the body, but it has to perform an important office, upon the due performance of which depends much of the health of the person. Its work appears to be of a twofold character: first, to carry off the waste products of the blood in the form of perspiration; second, to aid the lungs in absorbing oxygen; and both of these it does by means of the pores.

3. The sweat, or perspiration, is of two kinds; (i) that which appears in the form of drops upon the surface of the skin, and which follows upon violent exertion or mental emotion; (ii) that which passes off constantly, yet imperceptibly, and is called insensible perspiration. This can be detected readily by placing a large, cool, dry glass over the hand. In a short time the glass will be covered with moisture – this is the condensed vapour which has passed from the pores.

The quantity of perspiration varies with the temperature of the atmosphere, being more in hot weather than in cold, and with the state of the blood and nervous condition of the person. It is, however, always considerable.

4. The perspiration, whether insensible or sensible, contains fatty matters, and other waste products of the blood. If these are suffered to remain on the surface of the skin, they mix with the portions of dirt which necessarily adhere to the skin, and effectually seal up the mouths of the pipes.

5. The great use of the skin, then, is to carry off the waste matters of the blood, and to allow the passage of air into the system, and so to assist in preventing oxygen starvation. How important, then, that its action should not be interfered with! Its action is interfered with when, by the accumulation of dirt, or by exposure to cold, the pores are stopped up. Some idea may be formed of the evil which may result to health if the pores are stopped up by comparing the blood in the heart to the water in the cistern, the arteries and veins to the pipes which convey the water through all parts of the house, and the pores of the skin to the drain-pipes which convey the dirty water away from the house. Now suppose the water which has become foul by the washing of dishes, clothes, &c., instead of being allowed to run down the drain-pipes, was directed back to the cistern, very soon the whole of the water in the cistern would be

totally unfit for use. In some such way as this the blood in its passage round the body gets impure, and these impurities are in a great measure got rid of by means of the pores of the skin: if, however, these natural drain-pipes are stopped up, the impurities return again into the circulation, and thus render the blood unfit for use. This evil can in a great measure be prevented by cleanliness.

6. To insure the proper action of the skin, it is necessary to wash it constantly. The washing should not be confined to the face, neck, and hands, but should be applied to the whole body. It is not sufficient simply to wet the skin, it must be washed with soap, and the water should be lukewarm, at least now and then. In a word, there ought to be a free use made of the bath. If there is a public bath in the neighbourhood it should be used as often as possible, or its place supplied by a bath at home. It is not necessary to have a bath-room to enjoy a bath; very few houses are furnished with these luxuries. All that is needed to enjoy a bath is a piece of old carpet to stand on, and to keep the floor from getting wet, a pail of water, a piece of sponge or flannel, and two dry towels. A little care will be required in the use of the water, so as not to splash the furniture in the room, and a little self-denial, so as to rise in time to have the bath before any person is about.

7. After the skin has been washed, it should be well rubbed. There is no fear of wearing it away; only that part which it is intended should be removed – viz., the epidermis – will come off, and this is necessary, in order to keep the skin in good working condition. Whenever the skin cannot perform its proper work, some other organ has to do the work for it, and, of course, may be overworked, and ultimately break down. Thus the skin, by absorbing oxygen and excreting water in the form of perspiration, partakes of the nature of both lungs and kidneys. It is clear, therefore, that if these offices are not performed there must be more work for those organs. The work may be too great for them to accomplish, and if not done a loss of health will be the result. Hence it is impossible to overrate the importance of attention to the matter of cleanliness of person.

8. Apart from the duty of cleanliness, there is an enjoyable feeling experienced after a bath which is in itself an ample reward for the

trouble taken. Those persons who are in the habit of using water freely are quite at a loss to understand how it is that any one can endure dirt; and yet there are many men and women who seldom wash their whole body, and there are many children who dislike being washed. When the operation of washing is being performed, an abundance of water should be used; idleness ought never to keep us from fetching whatever may be necessary. Those persons who are in the habit of washing the body constantly are better able to do their work than those who have only a 'lick and a promise', and, at the same time, they have a great deal more enjoyment.

QUESTIONS ON LESSON XXIX

1. Of what does the skin consist?
2. Describe the pores.
3. What is the office of the skin?
4. What are the two kinds of perspiration?
5. What determines the amount of perspiration?
6. What does the perspiration contain?
7. What, then, is one of the first uses of the skin?
8. To insure the proper action of the skin, the pores must be kept open. How can this be done?
9. What other benefits attend the use of the bath?

Joseph Hassell, *Lessons in Domestic Economy for Elder Girls*, c. 1890

To the Little Ones

Children who drill
Seldom are ill,
For sinking, tiptoeing, and right and left going,
And shooting, and clapping, and measured-out tapping,
Strengthen their limbs,
Drive away whims,
Make faces shine brightly, make spines grow uprightly;
So, I suppose,
Illness all goes!

Children who learn
Bodies to turn,
And bodies to bend low, and noddles to send low,
And elbows to fetch out, and fingers to stretch out,
Seldom look pale,
Delicate, frail,
And seldom are sulky, and seldom too bulky,
And seldom are spiteful, but always delightful;
So dears, I still,
Beg you to drill!

Jennett Humphreys, *Laugh and Learn*, 1890.

THE BUNDLE OF STICKS

There was once a Farmer who had four very quarrelsome sons. To his great sorrow, he saw that they were far more ready to fall out with each other than to make friends.

One day, when he was very ill and thought he was about to die, he called them to his bedside and said –

'My sons, I shall soon have to leave you for ever. Before we part, I wish to give you some good advice.'

Turning to his youngest son, he said –

'Fetch here a bundle of sticks.'

The young man did so.

'Now,' said the old man, 'each of you try to break the bundle.'

The four sons , one after another, used their utmost strength, and tried in every way to break the bundle, but they failed to do so. It resisted all their efforts.

'Untie the bundle,' said their Father, 'and then break the sticks one by one.'

This was an easy thing to do, and in a few minutes all the sticks lay broken on the ground.

Pointing to the sticks, the Father said –

'My sons, learn from this little incident a lesson which may be of service to you all through life. Not one of you could break the sticks while they remained tied in a bundle, but a child could easily break them one by one. When you are friends, and acting towards each other like brothers you will be strong to help one another and to defend one another; but when you quarrel and refuse to be friends, others will easily get the better of you.'

MORAL: Union is strength.

My Book of Fables, c. 1895.

NEVER LOITER

A little boy, with a parcel in his hand, was one day walking along a country road. He had three miles to go, and the sun was very bright and warm.

He heard the birds singing in the trees, and saw the butterflies flitting about from flower to flower. Everything tempted him to loiter by the way.

Yet he walked along very quickly, thinking that the faster he walked the sooner he would be at home. As he went on his way, he heard a cart coming behind him.

As it came up to him, the driver stopped, and, having found out where the boy was going, kindly asked him to jump up beside him.

The boy was very glad to do so; and as they drove along, the driver, a good old farmer, began to talk with him. 'Do you know why I asked you to ride with me?' said he. 'No,' said the boy.

'Well, then, my boy, let me tell you. I saw you walking along very fast, and doing your duty, and so I asked you to ride.

'If I had seen you, with that parcel in your hand, wasting your time playing or idling by the way, I should not have asked you. I like to help those only whom I see doing their duty.'

Boys! think of what the old farmer said. Wherever you may be, whatever you may be doing, never idle or play when you have work to do.

The New Royal Readers, No. II. c. 1885.

The Doctor

Oh, do not fear the doctor;
He comes to make you well,
To nurse you like a tender flower,
And pleasant tales to tell;
He brings the bloom back to your cheek,
The blithe blink to your eye, –
An't were not for the doctor,
My bonnie bairn might die.

Oh, who would fear the doctor,
His powder or his pill –
You just a wee bit swallow take,
And there's an end of ill.
He'll make yousleep sound as a top,
And rise up like a fly, –
An't were not for the doctor,
My bonnie bairn might die.

HELPING GRANNIE

A kind man is the doctor,
As many poor folk ken;
He spares no toil by day or night
To ease them of their pain;
And oh, he loves the bairnies well
And grieves whene'er they cry, –
An't were not for the doctor,
My bonnie bairn might die.

Book of Juvenile Poetry, 1864.

VERY IGNORANT PEOPLE

I would have everybody able to read, and write, and cipher; indeed, I don't think a man can know too much; but mark you, the knowing of these things is not education; and there are millions of your reading and writing people who are as ignorant as neighbour Norton's calf, that did not know its own mother. This is as plain as the nose of your face, if you only think a little. To know how to read and write is like having tools to work, but if you don't use these tools, and your eyes, and your ears too, you will be none the better off. Everybody should know what most concerns him and makes him most useful. If cats can catch mice and hens can lay eggs, they know the things which most suits what they were made for. It is little use for a horse to know how to fly, it will do well enough if it can trot. A man on a farm ought to learn all that belongs to farming, a blacksmith should study a horse's foot, a dairymaid should be well up in skimming the milk and making the butter, and a labourer's wife should be a good scholar in the sciences of boiling and baking, washing and mending; and John Ploughman ventures to say that those men and women who have not learned the duties of their callings are very ignorant people, even if they can tell the Greek name for a crocodile, or write a poem on a black beetle. It is too often very true –

'Jack has been to school
To learn to be a fool.'

[71]

When a man falls into the water, to know how to swim will be of more use to him than all his mathematics, and yet how very few boys learn swimming! Girls are taught dancing and French when stitching and English would be a hundred per cent more use to them. When men have to earn their livings, in these hard times, a good trade and industrious habits will serve their turn a world better than all the classics in Cambridge and Oxford; but who nowadays advocates practical training at our schools? Schoolmasters would go into fits if they were asked to teach poor people's boys to hoe potatoes and plant cauliflowers, and yet school boards would be doing a power of good if they did something of the sort. If you want a dog to be a pointer or a setter, you train him accordingly: whyever don't they do the same with men? It ought to be 'every man for his business, and every man master of his business'. Let Jack and Tom learn geography by all means, but don't forget to teach them how to black their own boots, and put a button on to their own trousers; and as for Jane and Sally, let them sing and play the music if they like, but not till they can darn a stocking and make a shirt.

C. H. Spurgeon, *John Ploughman's Talk, or Plain Advice for Plain People*, c. 1890.

THE THREE LITTLE PIGS

Three little pigs once lived in a sty with an old sow.

They were so small that they could only say 'wee-wee', while the old sow could give a good loud grunt.

Now, one of the little pigs thought they ought all to try to grunt, for it made them seem so very small to say only 'wee-wee'.

So they all tried to grunt, and never said 'wee-wee'.

They tried so long and so hard that they got quite thin, and were all skin and bone.

At last they were quite ill with trying to do what they could not do.

They were too weak to say 'wee-wee' now, and one day they all three died.

Little folks, like little pigs, must not think they are as wise as old ones.

Some little folks think they know best what is good for them, and make a great noise if they do not get just what they want.

You must think of the little pigs who might have lived to grunt if they had not thought they were quite able to do it when they could only say 'wee-wee'.

New Standard Story Books, *c.* 1880.

Diddle-um, Daddle-um

How is your father, my diddle-um, daddle-um?
How is your mother, my diddle-um day?
How is your sister, my diddle-um, daddle-um?
How is your brother, my diddle-um day?

Do not call me, sir, your diddle-um, daddle-um!
Do not call me, sir, your diddle-um day!
I will not be, sir, your diddle-um, daddle-um!
I will not be, sir, your diddle-um day!
Nay! Nay!

Hey! Highty-tighty, my diddle-um, daddle-um!
How you are flighty, my diddle-um day!
Bid you good-nighty, my diddle-um, daddle-um!
So out of sighty, my diddle-um day!

Then I shall cry me, my diddle-um, daddle-um!
Then I shall die me, my diddle-um day!
Come and be by me, my diddle-um, daddle-um!
Kiss me, and try me, my diddle-um day!
Ay! Ay!

Jennett Humphreys, *Laugh and Learn*, 1890.

[73]

Polly's Pie

When Mary Ann was cooking once,
Our Polly made a pie;
She took some flour and water,
And some butter standing nigh;
And then she took some sugar, for
She says she likes things sweet,
And sprinkled on the rolling-board
All that she didn't eat.

She rolled it out a long, long time,
With salt a little bit;
She dropped it four times on the floor,
And once she stepped on it.
She doesn't think pie-plates of tin
Are pretty, so she took
A small, red flower-pot saucer,
Which was better for the cook.

She filled her pie with half a pear,
Two raisins, and a date;
Then put it in the oven, and
Forgot it till quite late.
It was not burned, for Mary Ann
Had taken care of that;
So Polly gave a party to
The chickens and the cat.

Chambers's Recitations for the Children, selected by
R. C. H. Morison, *c.* 1900.

THE NEW DOLL

Jane Day had a new doll; she had been to see her aunt, and her aunt gave the doll to her on her birthday. It was made of wax, with blue eyes and brown hair. It had wax arms, and wax legs and feet.

When she had had it a few days, she did not take as much care of it as when it was new: she did not put it by in the box which had been made for her to keep it in, when she left off play.

One day, when she had left it in this way on a chair, a boy came in to the room where it was; he took up the doll, and as he did not know the right way to hold it, he let it fall and broke it. So Jane Day had no nice doll to play with; but she said:

'The next time I have a doll, or a nice toy, I will not let it lie in the way; but I will take care and put it by when I do not want it; and then when I do want it, I shall have it to play with.'

Mrs Barwell, *Little Lessons for Little Learners in Words of One Syllable, c.* 1870.

GIVE HEED TO LITTLE THINGS

Two men were at work one day in a yard where ships are built. They were hewing a piece of timber to put into a ship. It was a small piece, and not worth much. As they cut off the chips, they found a worm – a little worm, not more than half an inch long.

'This bit of wood is wormy,' said one; 'shall we put it in?'

'I do not know,' said the other. 'Yes, I think it may go in. Of course, it will never be seen.'

'That may be; but there may be other worms in it, and in course of time they may destroy the hull.'

'No, I think not. To be sure, the piece of timber is not worth much; yet I do not wish to lose it. But, come, never mind the worm: we have seen only one. Put it in.'

And so the faulty bit of wood was put in. The ship was built and launched. She went to sea, and for ten years she did well. But at last she grew weak and rotten, for her timbers were very much eaten by worms.

However, the captain of the ship thought he would try to get her home. He had a costly cargo of silks and tea in the ship, and very many passengers.

During the voyage home a storm came on. The ship, for a while, climbed up the high waves, and then plunged down, creaking and rolling from side to side. At last she sprang a leak.

They had two pumps, and the men worked at them day and night; but the water came in faster than they could pump it out. The ship filled with water, and went down under the blue waves, with all the people and all the goods on board.

Oh, what a loss was there of life and of goods! and all because that little bit of timber, with the worm in it, was put in when the ship was built.

How much harm may be done by a little worm! And how much harm a man may do when he is not faithful even in the smallest thing!

Chambers's Expressive Readers, Book II, 1892.

The Factory Child's Hymn

I love to think of happy heav'n,
The city of our God;
Where all his little ones are giv'n,
A safe and blest abode.

When to my work, through cold and sleet,
I haste, with feet all bare,
I think upon the golden street,
And shining sunshine there.

And as I run with eager pace
Where'er the men desire,
I think, how wonderful the place
Where children never tire.

And when the noise is loud and long
Of engines ever near,
I think, how beautiful the song
Which angel children hear!

And I am happy all the day,
Whatever task is given,
Because I know this is the way
God trains my soul for heaven.

Within the busy factory hall
He bids me serve him well;
And then, for Jesus' sake, I shall
With him in glory dwell.

Though some dear children's journey there
Less rough and steep may be,
They are not more our Father's care,
Nor better loved than me.

The Illustrated Book of Songs for Children, c. 1863.

Alone in the Dark

She has taken out the candle,
She has left me in the dark;
From the window not a glimmer,
From the fireplace not a spark.

I am frightened as I'm lying
All alone here in my bed,
And I've wrapped the clothes as closely
As I can around my head.

There are birds out on the bushes,
In the meadow lies the lamb;
How I wonder if they're ever
Half as frightened as I am;

If they shake like me, and shiver
When they happen to awake,
With the dark sky all around them,
Ere the day begins to break.

But what is it makes me tremble?
And why should I fear the gloom?
I am certain there is nothing
In the corners of the room.

When the candle burned so brightly,
I could see them every one;
Are they changed to something fearful,
Only just because it's gone?

Though I speak, and no one answers,
In the quiet of the night,
Though I look, and through the blackness
Cannot see one gleam of light;

Still I know there's One who seeth
In the night as in the day,
For to Him the darkness dreary
Is as bright as noontide ray.

And perhaps while I am trying
How my foolish face to hide,
There is one of His good angels
Standing watching at my side.

Then I'll turn and sleep more soundly,
When one little prayer I've prayed;
For there's nothing in the darkness
That should make a child afraid.

Hymns and Rhymes for Children, c. 1875.

Child's Evening Hymn

The busy day is nearly done,
The dark, still night is coming on;
I'll pray Almighty God to keep
His care around me while I sleep.

I fear I have not been so good
In all things as I know I should;
Not so obedient, nor so mild,
Nor humble, as becomes a child.

Lord! if another day I see,
Teach me a better child to be;
For Thou, who mak'st the birds Thy care,
Wilt listen to an infant's prayer.

The Illustrated Spelling Book, c. 1855.

THURSDAY

The Good Boy

O, what a very pretty sight
It is to see the sun shine bright,
I'll get up now and say my prayers,
Be washed, and drest, and go down stairs;

How very good of God to keep
Me here in safety while I sleep,
And good to send me food each day,
And strength, to run about and play;

But breakfast is not ready yet,
So I my pretty book will get;
I'll try and please Mamma today,
And perfectly my lessons say.

Louisa Watts, *Pretty Little Poems for Pretty Little People*, 1846.

Primrose Gathering

Awake, dearest Auntie, and open your door;
The sun has been shining this hour or more.
You promised last night in the morning you'd go,
And show little Harry where primroses grow.
I've wash'd my round face, and I've comb'd my brown hair;
The birds are awake, and the weather is fair.
My dear little basket I'll take with me, too;
I like it because 'twas a present from you.
We'll fill it with blossoms all pick'd in their prime,
With garlands of hawthorn and cushions of thyme;
With daffodils yellow, and hyacinths blue;
And the best and the sweetest shall all be for you.
Make haste, dearest Auntie, and open your door;
I got up when the sun did, or rather before,
And I thought you'd be ready an hour ago,
To show little Harry where primroses grow.

Little Poems for Little Readers, c. 1870.

LESSONS ON PLANTS

THE FLOWER: LESSON 1

Teacher. What is this?
Pupils. A flower.

A perfect flower has four principal parts: you must try and find out these parts. What do you observe in these? (Teacher holds up a wall-flower and a primrose. Perhaps the children will say 'the flower', or 'yellow part', or 'the leaves'.) These coloured leaves of the flower form what is called the blossom. (Corolla is the scientific term, but it is most desirable in Infant Schools for the poor not to give a technical name, when any other can be found.) What is the first part of the flower that I am to write down on the slate?

The blossom.

What other part do you see as I hold up these flowers?

Some green leaves at the bottom of the blossom.

Are they green in the wall-flower?

No.

(The teacher should have a variety of flowers.)

But they are most frequently green. What use do these little leaves seem to be to the blossom?

They hold it.

What do you call the vessel that holds the tea you drink?

A cup.

And the part of the flower that holds the blossom is called the cup. (Calyx.) What shall I now write under the blossom?

The cup.

Now observe what I do to this flower, and tell me.

You have pulled off the blossom and the cup.

I did this in order that you might see what was within them. What do you find there?

A little thing in the middle with a round ball at the top.

That little thread-like thing in the middle is called the pistil. Repeat this word together. What shall I write down?

The pistil.

Now we will look for the pistils in the other flowers. Where shall I find them?
In the middle within the blossom.
Do you see anything besides the pistil within the blossom?
Yes, several little things like threads round the pistil.
These are called stamens. Repeat this word together. Let us find out the stamens in the other flowers. What shall I write on the slate?
Stamens.
How many parts are written down?
Four.
What are the four things which I have written on the slate?
The four principal parts of a flower.
Repeat them over together. Name each part as I touch it. You shall tell me now where each part is placed in the flower. Where do you find the pistil?
Within the blossom, in the middle.
Where do you find the stamens?
Within the blossom and round the pistil.
Where is the blossom?
Round the stamens and pistil.
Where is the cup?
On the outside of the blossom at the bottom.
What part is most carefully protected?
The pistil.
How is the pistil protected?
All the other parts of the flower are placed around it.
Why is it carefully guarded?
You said, teacher, that it was a very important part of the flower.
Can you tell me when it is that the blossom and cup still more carefully guard the pistil and stamens by being folded around them?
When the flower is in bud.
When do your mothers take most care of you, and are most afraid of any harm coming to you?
When we are little babies.
Yes, when you are young and weak, then your mothers take most care of you, and try to keep you from all harm, and when the pistil and stamens are very young and tender, they are beautifully covered and folded up within the blossom and cup. Look at this

bud. See how nicely the leaves are folded round the pistil, sheltering it from cold and wet. Who made this pretty flower?

God.

Do not use that word lightly, think of what you are saying, and speak with reverence; the great God who made the world we live in, the sun, and the moon, and the stars, made also this little flower; and what, dear children, does the examination of this little flower teach us about the great God?

That he takes care of what he makes.

And what does the Bible teach us – if he takes care of the flowers, what will he do for us?

Much more will he care for us.

Now tell me what you have learnt to-day about a flower.

We have learnt its four principal parts.

What are they?

The blossom, cup, pistil, stamens.

What more did you learn?

Where the parts are placed.

Tell me where each part is placed.

The blossom is placed round the stamens and pistil. The cup is placed on the outside of the blossom at the bottom. The pistil is placed within the blossom, in the middle. The stamens are placed within the blossom and round the pistil.

What lesson did you learn from the consideration of the flower?

That God takes care of all his works.

Model Lessons for Infant School Teachers and Nursery Governesses, by the Author of 'Lessons on Objects', 1842.

CLOTHES – A FABLE

A number of little boys and girls were one day sitting under a tree in a sunny meadow. They had been playing all the morning, and were tired.

They began to talk about their clothes. 'See!' said one of the boys, 'what a nice new hat I have got! and then my blue jacket and trousers – have you ever seen anything nicer?'

'Well,' replied a little girl, 'my hat cost a great deal more than yours. Then it has got a feather in it. And look at my dress and mantle too! My dress cost a great deal of money.' – 'Not so much as my jacket did,' answered the boy; 'of that I am quite sure.'

'You need not talk so much about your clothes,' said a caterpillar, that was creeping under the hedge; 'they are all second-hand, and have all been worn by some creature or other, before they came to you. Why, that silk of yours, young lady, first wrapped up a worm just like me.' – 'There! what have you to say to that?' cried the little boy.

'And the feather,' chirped a bird from a branch of the tree, 'was stolen from a friend of mine. A cruel man shot him, then tore off his wing and sold it to a hatter; and there it is now – in your hat!'

'Aha!' repeated the boy, 'what can you say to that? At any rate, *my* clothes were never worn by birds or crawling worms.'

'That is true,' said a sheep that had just come up; 'but they were worn by my brothers and sisters long before they came upon your back. The hat, too, that you are so proud of, is made of the covering of the silk-worm; and the poor little calves had to give up their skins before they could be made into shoes for your feet.'

'Is that so?' said the boy. 'Then it seems to me there is nothing to be proud of. We owe all these things to what are called the lower animals.'

'If all this is true,' added the little girl, 'I will not boast of my clothes again. Besides, after all, it was my father and mother who gave them to me; and, if I think about my clothes at all, I should only think how good and kind my parents have been to me.' – 'Well, I suppose you are right,' said the boy.

And the children stopped all this silly talk about clothes, and began their pleasant games again.

Chambers's Graduated Readers, Book III, 1897.

Manners

Mother says that she must pay
Twopence at our schools
To teach us manners and of good
Society the rules.

We must not bounce into the room,
We mustn't scuttle out,
Nor ever bang the drawing-room door;
And girls must never shout.

There's many things for boys to learn
Before they will behave,
They must not ask old gentlemen
Why their heads are shaved.

They always ought to scrape their boots
And wipe them on the mat;
They should not steal the ginger-bread,
And say it was the cat.

You should answer when you're spoken to,
At least if you are able.
The place for elbows, you must know,
Is not upon the table.

Then mother ends her lecture with
'Remember, if you can,
This simple little saying, that,
"'Tis manners maketh man."'

Tit-Bits Monster Recitation Book, c. 1900.

CHARLIE ON THE BRIDGE

'Now,' said Charlie Piper's mother to him, as he went out of the door to go to school, '*don't you harbour that* THIEF *today – don't forget!*'

'No, mother, I will not,' said Charlie Piper.

What! a boy of Charlie Piper's age harbour a thief! One would think he could have nothing to do with thieves. Yes, one would suppose so; yet there was one thief so sly that he used to slip into Charlie's good graces, and Charlie used to go with him. He well knew that his doing so grieved his mother, and hurt his own credit, yet it was some time before he had firmness enough to take a manly stand against him.

On he goes until he gets almost over the bridge, when he stops a minute to watch the little fishes darting about in the water below. He almost wished that he was a fish. He was sure fishes must be very happy, with nothing to do the livelong day but *play* in the water.

Charlie well knew he had not a moment to spare on the bridge, or he would be late; but still he kept stopping there. In fact, his old friend the thief was beside him, ready to steal his priceless moments. So he kept stopping, and stopping, thinking about the fishes, and saying, 'Oh, it is too pleasant here to be cooped up in that old school-room!' until, all at once, his mother's words, '*Don't forget!*' rushed into his mind.

He started up from lounging on the rails of the bridge, threw back his arms, as much as to say, 'Hands off, Mr Thief!' and took to his heels. He got to the school, and had the good fortune to be just in time.

'Good,' said Charlie, looking as glad as he could be. 'I have made my escape this time – I have! Goodbye, Mr Thief! you and I will, I hope, have no more dealings with one another.'

Charlie was as good as his word. From this time, instead of being a boy always used to *delay*, he became the very soul of promptness. After this, that THIEF DELAY kept at a distance from and at last never came near him. Delay is fitly called a thief, for it robs us of one of our best treasures, *time*.

The Grade Lesson Book, First Standard, *c.* 1870.

LESSONS ON DOMESTIC ECONOMY

LESSON XLII · ON MINDING BABY

Most girls have been called upon to mind their baby brother or sister. Now this 'minding baby' is a very important work, and one which every elder sister should endeavour to do well. To assist her to become a good nurse, or minder of babies, the following hints are given. The lady who drew them up was an excellent nurse herself, and a lover of babies. Here is what she says on the subject.

1. You must take care that baby is not startled by loud sudden noises; all the more you must not wake it in this way out of its sleep. Noises which would not frighten you frighten baby. Many a sick child has been killed in this way.

2. You must be careful about its food: about being strict to the minute for feeding it: not giving it too much at a time (if baby is sick after its food you have given it too much). Neither must it be under-fed. Above all, never give it unwholesome food, nor anything at all to make it sleep, unless the doctor orders it.

3. Baby who is weaned requires to be fed often, regularly, and not too much at a time.

I knew a mother whose baby was in great danger one day from convulsions. It was about a year old. She said she had wished to go to church; and so, before going, had given it its three meals in one. Was it any wonder that the poor thing had convulsions? I have known a little girl, not more than five years old, whose mother had to go to a great distance every day, and who was trusted to feed and take care of her little brother under a year old. And she always did it right. She always did what mother told her. A stranger coming in the cottage one day said, 'You will burn baby's mouth.' 'Oh no,' she said, 'I always burn my own mouth first.'

4. You must be careful of baby. When I say be careful of baby, I don't mean always have it in your arms. If the baby is old enough, and the weather warm enough for it to have some heat in itself, it is much better for a child to crawl about than to be always in its little

nurse's arms; and it is much better for it to amuse itself than to have her always making noises to it.

I think there is a great deal too much of amusing children now, and not enough of letting them amuse themselves. Never distract a child's attention. If it is looking at one thing don't show it another: and so on.

5. At the same time, dullness, and especially want of light, is worse for children than it is for you.

A child was once brought up quite alone in a dark room by persons who wished to conceal its being alive. It never saw any one, except when it was fed; and though it was treated perfectly kindly, it grew up an idiot. This you will easily guess.

Plenty of light, and sunlight particularly, is necessary to make a child active, and merry, and clever. But of all things do not burn baby's brains out by letting the sun bake its head when out, especially in its little cart, on a hot summer's day.

Never leave a child in the dark; and let the room it lives in be always as light as possible, and as sunny. Except of course, when the doctor tells you to darken the room, which he will do in some children's illnesses.

6. Do you know that one-half of all the nurses in service are girls of from five to twenty years old? You see you are very important little people. Then there are all the girls who are nursing mother's baby at home; and in all these cases it seems pretty nearly to come to this, that baby's health for its whole life depends upon you, girls, more than upon anything else. Now most of you care about the baby, and want to make it grow up well and happy, if you knew how.

7. The main want of baby is always to have fresh air.

You can make baby ill by keeping the room where it sleeps tight shut up, even for a few hours.

You can kill baby when it is ill by keeping it in a hot room with several people in it, and all the doors and windows shut. This is the case most particularly when the child has something the matter with its lungs and breathing.

But,

8. Take care not to let a draught blow upon a child, especially a sick child. You may give baby a chill which will kill it (by letting a draught blow upon it when it is being washed, for instance, and chilling its whole body, though only for a moment) without giving it fresh air at all; and depend upon this, the less fresh air you give to its lungs, and the less water you give its skin, the more liable it will be to colds and chills. A sick baby's skin is often cold, even when the room is quite close. Then you must air the room, and put hot flannels or hot bottles (not too hot) next the baby's body, and give it warm food.

But I have often seen a nurse doing just the contrary: namely, shutting up every chink and throwing a great weight of bed-clothes over the child, which makes it colder, as it has no heat in itself. You would just kill a feverish child by doing this.

9. Remember to keep baby clean. I dare say you know that to keep every spot of baby's body clean, and never to let any pore of its tender skin be stopped up by dirt, or unwashed perspiration, is the only way to keep baby happy and well. It may be a great deal of trouble; but it is a great deal more trouble to have baby sick.

The safest thing is to wash baby all over once or twice a day in luke-warm water. There may be danger in washing a child's feet and legs only. There never can be in washing it all over.

10. Baby's clothes should be changed oftener than yours, because of the greater quantity which baby perspires. If you clothe baby in filth, what can you expect but that it will be ill? Its clothes must never be light, but light and warm. Baby, if not properly clothed, feels sudden changes in the weather much more than you do. Baby's bed-clothes must be clean oftener than yours.

Now, can you remember the things you have to mind for baby? There is –

Fresh air.

Proper warmth.

Cleanliness for its little body, its clothes, its bed, its room and house.

Feeding with proper food at regular times.

Not startling it, or shaking either its little body, or its little nerves.

Light and cheerfulness.

Proper clothes in bed and up.

And management in all these things.

Bear in mind that it is as easy to put out a sick baby's life as it is to put out the flame of a candle. Ten minutes' delay in giving it food may make the difference.

QUESTIONS ON LESSON XLII

1. Why should the baby not be startled by noise?
2. How often do young children need feeding?
3. What is meant by being careful of baby?
4. Why should you be cheerful with baby?
5. Why are nurses important persons?
6. Why should baby have plenty of fresh air?
7. Why should you be careful not to let baby be in a draught?
8. Show the importance of keeping baby clean.

Joseph Hassell, Lessons in Domestic Economy for Elder Girls, c. 1890.

NEVER TELL LIES

That wicked spirit, the devil, who was a liar from the first, is the father of all liars. That is, as a child is like its father, so is a liar like the devil, and may be called his child.

Surely you would not wish to be like the devil, that very wicked being, who cheated our first parents by a lie and thus brought death and sin, and sorrow and trouble, into the world. Never be a child of the devil.

Besides, there is something in deceit that is very unfair. We do not like any person to deceive us; then why should we deceive him? This is not doing to others as we would have them do to us.

Liars are wicked persons, who having first done something that is bad, then attempt to hide or cover their sin by a falsehood. Thus they make their sin very bad indeed.

It is better to confess the wrong at once. A boy had chopped a young tree. His father asked him if he did it. He said, Father, I cannot tell a lie, I did it. This was noble: and his father forgave him. That boy became a great man.

God is the God of truth. He hates all liars. In the Bible we find some awful judgments on liars; and God hates all liars now as much as He did then. And He will always hate all liars.

And God, who can cast both soul and body into hell, has said that all liars shall be sent to that sad place, where the devil and his angels are.

Be sure that you always speak the truth. Never tell a lie; no, not to gain a purse of gold. Truth is worth more than gold or silver.

If anyone is known to tell lies, no one will believe him; no, not when he does speak the truth. But if we always speak the truth, all will trust us, and honour us too.

The New Class Books for Sabbath Schools: Second Reading Lessons, *c.* 1875.

The Cold-Water Boy

Hurrah, for a splash!
Come, give me a dash,
With the water all clear and cold;
It makes me so bright,
So active and light,
'Tis better than silver and gold.

Oh, what should I do,
Dear mother, if you
Never wash'd me so sweet and so clean?
Come, give me a splashing;
It is so refreshing,
All the day I would like to stay in.

I never would cry,
Nor halloo – not I –
Unless 'twere for joy and for glee;
I love the good splashing,
And plunging, and dashing:
Hurrah the cold water for me!

Little Poems for Little Readers, c. 1870.

I WILL THINK OF IT

'I will think of it.' It is easy to say this; but do you know what great
things have come from thinking?

We cannot see our thoughts, or hear, or taste, or feel them; and
yet what mighty power they have!

Sir Isaac Newton was seated in his garden on a summer evening,
when he saw an apple fall from a tree. He began to *think*, and, in
trying to find out why the apple fell, discovered how the earth, sun,
moon, and stars are kept in their places.

A boy named James Watt sat quietly by the fireside, watching the lid of the tea-kettle as it moved up and down. He began to *think*; he wanted to find out why the steam in the kettle moved the heavy lid.

From that time he went on thinking, and thinking; and when he became a man, he improved the steam-engine so much that it could, with the greatest ease, do the work of many horses.

When you see a steam-boat, a steam-mill, or a locomotive, remember that it would never have been built if it had not been for the hard thinking of some one.

A man named Galileo was once standing in the cathedral of Pisa, when he saw a chandelier swaying to and fro.

This set him *thinking*, and it led to the invention of the pendulum.

James Ferguson was a poor Scotch shepherd-boy. Once, seeing the inside of a watch, he was filled with wonder. 'Why should I not make a watch?' thought he.

But how was he to get the materials out of which to make the wheels and the mainspring? He soon found how to get them. He made the mainspring out of a piece of whalebone. He then made a wooden clock, which kept good time.

He also began to copy pictures with a pen, and portraits with oil-colours. In a few years, while still a small boy, he earned money enough to support his father.

When he became a man, he went to London to live. Some of the wisest men in England, and the king himself, used to attend his lectures. His motto was, 'I will *think* of it'; and he made his thoughts useful to himself and the world.

Children, when you have a difficult lesson to learn, don't feel discouraged, and ask someone to help you before helping your-selves. Think; and by thinking, you will learn how to think to some purpose.

Chambers's Graduated Readers, Book III, 1897.

GOOD AND BAD APPLES

One day Robert's father saw him playing with some bad boys. He had observed for some time a change for the worse in his son, and now he knew the cause. He was very sorry, but he said nothing to Robert at the time.

In the evening he brought from the garden six beautiful apples, put them on a plate, and gave them to Robert, who thanked him.

'You must lay them aside for a few days, that they may become mellow,' said the father. Robert cheerfully placed the plate with the apples in his mother's store-room.

Just as he was putting them away, his father laid on the plate a seventh apple, which was quite rotten, and he desired Robert to let it remain there.

'Father,' said Robert, 'the rotten apple will spoil all the others.'

'Do you think so? Why should not the sound apples rather make the bad one sound?' said his father. With these words he shut the door of the room.

Eight days afterward he asked his son to open the door and take out the apples. But what a sight was there! The six apples, which had been so sound and good, spread a bad smell through the room.

'O father!' cried he, 'did I not tell you that the rotten apple would spoil the good ones?'

'My boy,' said his father, 'have I not often told you that the company of bad children will make you bad? Yet you do not listen to me. I want you to learn a lesson from these apples. If you keep company with wicked boys, you will soon be like them.'

Robert did not forget the lesson. When any of his former play-fellows asked him to join in their games, he thought of the rotten apples, and refused to play with them.

The New Royal Readers, No. II, *c.* 1885.

The Skipping-Rope

Sweet Lilian with the skipping-rope,
You've won my heart from me,
You look so bright, young Lilian:
Says Lilian, 'One, two, three.'

Sweet Lilian with the skipping-rope,
My heart is in a fix,
For I'm in love with some one else:
Cries Lilian, 'Four, five, six.'

Sweet Lilian with the skipping-rope,
Say, will you not be mine?
Don't hit me with your skipping-rope:
Sings Lilian, 'Seven, eight, nine.'

Mrs Charles Heaton, *Routledge's Album for Children*, 1871.

DARE TO SAY, NO

'Will you go a-nutting with me this afternoon in Farmer Smith's plantation?' said William Johnson to Harry Drake.

'No!' replied Harry.

'Oh, you will surely go: the nuts are all ripe and ready for gathering, and Farmer Smith has gone to market. Come, do go.'

'No!' again said Harry.

'Can you say nothing but "No"?' asked William, who had fully expected to get Harry to go with him.

'We have no right on Farmer Smith's grounds; and that is why I say No!' replied Harry.

William went a-nutting alone; and Harry remained behind.

William was caught in the plantation by one of Farmer Smith's men, and was well whipped.

If all boys and girls learned to say No! when asked to do wrong, they would be saved from much trouble.

When play-mates tell you this or that
Is 'very nice to do,'
Consider well at first; and if
You think it wrong, say, No.

Be always gentle, but be firm:
Wherever you may go,
If you are asked to do what's wrong,
Don't fear to answer, No.

False friends may laugh and sneer at you,
Temptations round you flow,
But prove yourself right brave and true,
And firmly tell them, No.

True friends will honour you the more –
Ah, yes, and false ones too,
When they have learned you're not afraid
To stand and answer, No.

And when temptations rise within,
And plead to 'come' or 'go'
And do a wrong for just this once,
Be sure you answer, No.

There's many a little boy and girl,
And man and woman too,
Have gone to ruin and to death
For want of saying, No.

So, young or old, and great or small,
Wherever you may go,
Stand up for right, and nobly dare
To speak an honest No.

Royal Readers, No. II, Third Series, 1879.

AN ODD WAY OF CATCHING THEM

'When I was a boy at school,' said my grandfather, 'I was often very idle. Even during lessons I used to play with other boys as idle as myself. Of course we tried to hide this from the master, but one day we were fairly caught.

'"Boys," said he, "you must not be idle; – you must attend to your books. You do not know what you lose by being idle now. Youth is the time to learn. Any one of you who sees another boy looking off his book will please come and tell me."

'"Ah," thought I to myself, "there is Joe Smith, whom I don't like; I'll watch him, and if I see him look off his book, I'll tell." Not very long afterwards I saw Joe look off his book, and I at once marched up and told the master.

'"Indeed," said he; "how do you know he was idle?" – "Please, sir," said I, "I saw him." – "Oh, you did, did you; and where were *your* eyes on your book when you saw him?"

'I was fairly caught; the other boys laughed, and I hung my head, while the master smiled. I never watched for idle boys again.'

If we watch over our own conduct, and always do our own duty, we shall have no time to watch for faults or idleness in others.

The New Royal Readers, No. II, c. 1885.

What Good Cats Do

Old Cat What a cat I am! I have children nine;
Yes, all these little darlings are mine!
I purr all day long, and I purr all night;
What cat wouldn't that saw such a sight? –
Frisky, my dear, you're my first-born child:
Don't play with your whiskers, don't be so wild;
Sit still, and tell me what good cats do.
Frisky They mew.

Old Cat Was there ever such a kitten as that?
I'm afraid she'll never grow into a cat. –
Whitenose, my son, just put down your paws;
Stop biting and scratching, and draw in your claws:
Now tell me, sir, what good cats do?
Whitenose They mew.
Old Cat Alas! alas! oh, what have I done
To have such a thoughtless kit of a son? –
Softpaws, darling, I'm sure that you
Can tell your mother what good cats do.
Softpaws They mew.
Old Cat You stupid child, you! – Now, Tiny, my dear,
Speak up quite loud, so they all can hear,
And tell us quickly what good cats do.
Tiny They mew.
Old Cat Oh! was there ever so stupid a set?
I'm sure they know, but they always forget. –
Now, Spotty, my dear, do stop that frisking,
You're always jumping and boxing and whisking.
You can tell us what good cats do.
Spotty They mew.
Old Cat Why, this is dreadful! – Now, Grayeyes, my child,
Answer me right, or you'll drive me wild!
Don't say the same as your sisters and brothers,
And give such silly replies as the others.
Tell me now what the good cats do.
Grayeyes They mew.
Old Cat Was ever a mother cat so tried?
If I had a veil, my face I would hide. –
Blackears, my dear, you're mother's own kit;
You must have some of your mother's wit.
Come! you can tell us what good cats do!
Blackears They mew.
Old Cat It is truly amazing! – Kitty, my dear,
Fold your white paws down and prick up your ear.
Now tell me, darling, what good cats do.
Kitty They mew.

Old Cat I have one hope left! Rolypoly, 'tis you!
Tell me, my pet, what the good cats do.
Rolypoly They sit on their tails, with grave-looking faces;
They whisk not,
They frisk not;
They make no grimaces;
They train up their kittens the way they should go;
They think a great deal on the doings of rats,
And kill them all off, if they're *very* good cats.
Dear mother, was this what you wanted to know?
Old Cat Oh, yes, my darling! I thought that you
Could tell your mother what good cats do.
Come to my arms! You're my joy, my delight; –
As for the rest of you, out of my sight!
(*Kittens go off, weeping*)

The New Royal Readers, No. II, *c*. 1885.

THE TWO MEN AND THE BEAR

As two Men were walking through a wood they saw a Bear coming towards them. One of the men quickly climbed up a tree and hid himself among the branches. The other could not get out of the Bear's way in time, and seeing no chance of escape, he played the Bear a trick.

He had heard that a bear will not touch a dead body, so he at once fell flat upon the ground as if he were dead, and waited for the coming of the Bear. The animal came up very cautiously, smelled at the Man on the ground, and then passed on.

As soon as the Bear was out of sight the Man in the tree came down and asked his friend what the Bear had said to him.

'For,' said the coward, 'I noticed that he held his mouth very close to your ear.'

'He told me,' said the other, 'never again to travel with a friend who deserts me in the hour of danger.'

MORAL: Cowards think only of saving themselves.

My Book of Fables, c. 1895.

Where's Mother?

Bursting in from school or play,
This is what the children say,
Trooping, crowding, big and small,
On the threshold, in the hall –
Joining in the constant cry,
Ever as the days go by:
'Where's mother?'

From the weary bed of pain
This same question comes again;
From the boy with sparkling eyes,
Bearing home his earliest prize;

[105]

From the bronzed and bearded son,
Perils past and honours won:
'Where's mother?'

Burdened with a lonely task,
One day we may vainly ask
For the comfort of her face,
For the rest of her embrace;
Let us love her while we may,
Well for us that we can say:
'Where's mother?'

Mother, with untiring hands,
At the post of duty stands;
Patient, seeking not her own,
Anxious for the good alone
Of her children as they cry,
Ever as the days go by:
'Where's mother?'

Tit-Bits Monster Recitation Book, c. 1900.

HINTS AS TO THRIVING

Look most to your spending. No matter what comes in, if more goes
out you will always be poor. The art is not in making money, but in
keeping it; little expenses, like mice in a barn, when they are many,
make great waste. Hair by hair heads get bald. Straw by straw the
thatch goes off the cottage, and drop by drop the rain comes into the
chamber. A barrel is soon empty if the tap leaks but a drop a
minute. Chickens will be plucked feather by feather if the maid
keeps at it; small mites eat the cheese; little birds destroy a great deal
of wheat. When you mean to save, begin with your mouth; there are
many thieves down the red lane. The ale jug is a great waster. In all
other things keep within compass. In clothes choose suitable and
lasting stuff, and not tawdry fineries. To be warm is the main thing;

never mind the looks. Never stretch your legs further than your blankets will reach, or you will soon be cold. A fool may make money, but it needs a wise man to spend it. Remember it is easier to build two chimneys than to keep one going. If you give all to back and board there is nothing left for the savings bank. Fare hard and work hard while you are young, and you have a chance of rest when you are old.

Never indulge in extravagance unless you want to make a short cut to the workhouse. Money has wings of its own, and if you find it another pair of wings, wonder not if it flies fast.

> He that hath it, and will not keep it;
> He that wants it, and will not seek it;
> He that drinks, and is not dry,
> Shall want money as well as I.

If our poor people could only see the amount of money which they melt away in drink their hair would stand on end with fright. Why, they swallow rivers of beer, and seas of porter, and great big lakes of spirits and other fire waters. We should all be clothed like gentlemen and live like fighting cocks if what is wasted on fuddle could be sensibly used. We should need to get up earlier in the morning to spend all our money, for we should find ourselves suddenly made quite rich, and all that through stopping the drip of the tap. At any rate, you young people who want to get on in the world must make a point of dropping your half-pints, and settle in your spirits that no spirits shall ever settle you. Have your luxuries, if you must have them, after you have made your fortune, but just now look after your bread and cheese.

C. H. Spurgeon, *John Ploughman's Talk, or, Plain Advice for Plain People, c.* 1890.

Grandfather's Chair

I love, when the evenings are balmy and still,
And summer is smiling on valley and hill,
To see in the garden the little ones there,
All happy and smiling round grandfather's chair.

Such stories he tells them – such tales of delight –
Such wonders to dream of by day and by night,
It's little they're thinking of sorrow and care,
Their bright faces beaming round grandfather's chair.

And words, too, of wisdom fall oft from his tongue,
Dear lessons to cherish and treasure while young;
Bright things to remember when white is their hair,
And some of them sit in a grandfather's chair.

Ah! little ones, love him, be kind while you may,
For swiftly the moments are speeding away;
Not long the kind looks and the love you may share,
That beam on you now from a grandfather's chair.

Matthias Barr, *The Child's Garland of Little Poems*, *c.* 1870.

Song to a Baby

Sleep, baby, sleep!
Your father herds his sheep,
Your mother shakes the little tree
From which fall pretty dreams on thee.
Sleep, baby, sleep!

Sleep, baby, sleep!
The heavens are white with sheep,
For they are lambs, those stars so bright,
And the moon's the shepherd of the night.
Sleep, baby, sleep!

Sleep, baby, sleep!
And I'll give thee a sheep;
Which with its golden bell shall be
A pretty play-fellow for thee.
Sleep, baby, sleep!

Sleep, baby, sleep!
Go out and herd the sheep;
Go out you barking black dog go,
And waken not my baby so.
Sleep, baby, sleep!

*A Little Book for Little Readers, by the Editor of the
'Parting Gift', 1837.*

Fear of the Dark

I will not fear,
For God is near
Through the dark night,
As in the light;
And while I sleep,
Safe watch will keep.
Why should I fear
When God is near?

Hymns and Rhymes for
Children, c. 1875.

FRIDAY

Up in the Morning

'*Up in the morning!*' singeth the lark,
As it soars away over field and park;
Over the hills and the clouds so high,
To welcome the sun in the golden sky.

'*Up in the morning!*' hummeth the bee,
As it wanders away by the flower and tree,
While the dew lies bright on bud and bloom,
And the meadows are filled with sweet perfume.

'*Up in the morning!*' croweth the cock,
While the hens flutter down and around him flock;
'Up in the morning!' till woodland and hill
Re-echo his crowing so loud and shrill.

'*Up in the morning!*' bleateth the sheep,
As it rises to roam through the herbage deep,
And sips the drops of the crystal dew,
While the sun mounts up to the sky's deep blue.

'*Up in the morning!*' bellow the cows,
As on the rich grass of the meadows they browse,
Ere the sun has drunk the sweet dew up
From the fresh green blade and the daisy's cup.

Rise early, dear children, if you would grow strong;
Rise early, dear children, if you would live long:
The ways of the slothful for ever be scorning;
Be no sleep sluggards, but 'up in the morning!'

Royal Natural History Readers, No. I: *The Animals around Us*;
for Standard II, 1881.

THE OWL AND THE GRASSHOPPER

An Owl, who was sitting in a hollow tree, dozing away a long summer afternoon, was much disturbed by a rogue of a Grasshopper, singing in the grass below.

So far from moving away at the request of the Owl, or keeping quiet, the Grasshopper sang all the more, saying that honest people got their sleep at night.

The Owl waited in silence for a while, and then said to the Grasshopper: 'I ought to be angry with you, I suppose, my dear, for I confess I would rather sleep than listen to your singing. But if one cannot be allowed to sleep, it is something to be kept awake by such a pleasant little pipe as yours. And now it occurs to me that I have a nice drink with which to reward one who sings so sweetly. If you will take the trouble to come up, you shall have a drop. It will clear your voice nicely.'

The silly Grasshopper came hopping up to the Owl, who at once caught and killed him, and then finished her nap in comfort.

MORAL: Be not deceived by false praise.

My Book of Fables, c. 1895.

How Glad I Shall Be
When the Cuckoo is Singing

How glad I shall be when the cuckoo is singing,
When springtime is here, and the sunshine is warm;
For 'tis pleasant to tread where the bluebell is springing,
And lily-cups grow in their fairy-like form.
Then we shall see the loud twittering swallow,
Building his home 'neath the cottager's eaves;
The brown-headed nightingale quickly will follow,
And the orchard be grand with its blossoms and leaves.
The branches so gay will be dancing away,
Decked out in their dresses so white and so pink;
And then we'll go straying,
And playing
And Maying
By valleys, and hills, and the rivulet's brink.

How glad I shall be when the bright little daisies
Are peeping all over the meadows again;
How merry 'twill sound when the skylark upraises
His carolling voice o'er the flower-strewn plain.
Then the corn will be up, and the lambs will be leaping,
The palm with its buds of rich gold will be bent;
The hedges of hawthorn will burst from their sleeping,
All fresh and delicious with beauty and scent.
'Twill be joyous to see the young wandering bee,
When the lilacs are out, and laburnum boughs swell;
And then we'll go straying,
And playing
And Maying
By upland and lowland, by dingle and dell.

How glad I shall be when the furze-bush and clover
Stand up in their garments of yellow and red;
When the butterfly comes like a holiday rover,
And grasshoppers cheerily jump as we tread.
All the sweet, wild flowers then will be shining,
All the high trees will be covered with green;
We'll gather the rarest of blossoms for twining,
And garland the brow of some bonnie May Queen.
Like the branches so gay, we'll go dancing away,
With our cheeks in the sunlight, and voices of mirth;
And then we'll go straying,
And playing
And Maying,
And praise all the loveliness showered on earth.

Rhymes for Young Readers, from the Works of Eliza Cook, 1869.

SAY NO BAD WORDS

Children learn this bad habit by hearing others, and so they should not go in the way of wicked men or bad children, lest they learn their evil ways, and be like them.

Now it is written in the holy Word of God, Thou shalt fear this great and dreadful name, the Lord thy God. And again, Thou shalt not take the name of the Lord thy God in vain.

And yet there are wicked men who will when they are in anger, and when they are in sport, take the Name of the Most High in vain, in the most shameful and wicked manner.

Angels in the high heaven fear the Lord God; and the devils in hell tremble before him. All good men fear him, and they fear him much.

Is it not then very foolish and wicked to profane the name of the Most High? He could in one moment send such a wretched sinner into hell. And many have died saying bad words.

There is nothing which a boy or girl will sooner learn than bad words if they do not mind. And so be sure and mind that you do not.

Some boys are so foolish and wicked as to think that they are like men if they utter such bad words as some men do. This is an evil and foolish thing in all who do so.

Let all such know that the great God puts down in his book all the idle and wicked words that are said against the judgment day, and let them not think he will forget them, for he cannot forget such things.

Be careful, then, to avoid wicked men and wicked children. Never learn any of their bad words, but reprove those who use them, and then go away. For it is not good to be with such.

Our tongues were made not to curse and swear, but to bless the Lord who made us, and tell each other of what may be for our good.

The New Class Books for Sabbath Schools: Second Reading Lessons, *c.* 1875.

Charity

Do you see that old beggar who stands at the door?
Do not send him away – we must pity the poor.
Oh, see how he shivers! he's hungry and cold!
For people can't work when they grow very old.

Go set near the fire a table and seat:
And Betty shall bring him some bread and some meat.
I hope my dear children will always be kind,
Whenever they meet with the aged and blind.

A Poetry Book for Schools, 1879.

SYMPATHY

WINE IS A MOCKER

Wine is a mocker, strong drink is raging: and whosoever is deceived thereby is not wise. PROV. 20: 1.

Woe unto them that rise up early in the morning, that they may follow strong drink; that continue until night, till wine inflame them. ISA. 5: 11.

Look not thou upon the wine when it is red, when it giveth his colour in the cup, when it moveth itself aright. At the last it biteth like a serpent, and stingeth like an adder. PROV. 23: 31, 32.

Let us watch and be sober. I THESS. 5: 6.

Page for home framing in *The Friendly Visitor*, 1880.

THE LITTLE HERO

Once there was a little drummer-boy who was much liked by his officers. One day he was asked by the captain to drink a glass of rum. But he said, 'I am a temperance boy, and do not taste strong drink.'

'But you must take some now,' said the captain. 'You have been on duty all day, beating the drum and marching, and now you must not refuse.' But the boy stood firm.

The captain then turned to the major and said, 'Our little drummer is afraid to drink. He will never make a soldier.' – 'How is this?' said the major in a playful manner. 'Do you refuse to obey orders?'

'Sir,' said the boy, 'I have never refused to obey orders, and have tried to do my duty as a soldier; but I must refuse to drink rum, for I know it would do me harm.'

'Then,' said the major, in a stern tone of voice, in order to try him, 'I command you to take a drink; and you know it is death to disobey orders!'

The little fellow, fixing his clear blue eyes on the face of the officer, said, 'Sir, my father died a drunkard; and when I became a soldier I promised my mother that I would not taste a drop of rum, and I mean to keep my promise. I am sorry to disobey your orders, sir; but I would rather suffer anything than disgrace my mother, and break my pledge.'

Was not that a brave boy? He had learned when to say NO. The officers could not help being pleased at his conduct, and ever afterwards treated him with great kindness.

The New Royal Readers, No. II, *c.* 1885.

O Say, Busy Bee

O say, busy bee, whither now are you going,
Whither now are you going, to work, or to play?
'I am bound to the garden, where roses are blowing,
For I must be making sweet honey today.
Sweet honey, sweet honey,
For I must be making sweet honey today.'

O say, pretty dove, whither now are you flying,
Whither now are you flying, to London or Rome?
'I am bound to my nest, where my partner is sighing,
And waiting for me in my snug little home.
Little home, little home,
And waiting for me in my snug little home.'

So we, all so happy, while daily advancing
In wisdom and knowledge, in virtue and love,
Will sing on our way, in our learning rejoicing,
As brisk as the bee, and as true as the dove,
Will sing, will sing
As brisk as the bee, and as true as the dove.

John Curwen (ed.), *Songs and Tunes for Education*, 1861.

BEFORE YOU ARE FIFTEEN

Someone has suggested fifteen things that every girl can learn before she is fifteen. Not everyone can learn to play or sing or paint well enough to give pleasure to her friends, but the following accomplishments are within everybody's reach.

1. Shut the door, and shut it softly.
2. Keep your own room in tasteful order.
3. Have an hour for rising, and rise.
4. Learn to make bread as well as cake.
5. Never let a button stay off twenty-four hours.
6. Always know where your things are.
7. Never let a day pass without doing something to make somebody comfortable.
8. Never come to breakfast without a collar.
9. Never go about with your shoes unbuttoned.
10. Speak clearly enough for everybody to understand.
11. Never fidget or hum, so as to disturb others.
12. Never help yourself at the table before you pass the plate.
13. Be patient with the little ones, as you wish your mother to be with you.
14. Never keep anybody waiting.
15. Never fuss or fret.

The girl who has thoroughly learnt all this might almost be called a Mistress of Arts.

The Children's Friend, July 1899.

THE TWO GOATS

On a wild mountain, two goats met on a ledge just over a high cliff. The ledge was so narrow, that there was neither room for them to pass each other nor to turn round and go back.

A steep rock rose straight above them – a deep dark chasm lay below! What do you think the two goats did?

One of them with great care laid himself down on the narrow ledge, pressing as close to the rock as he could. Then the other goat gently and softly stepped over his friend, till, safely past him, he could lightly bound away.

The goat that had lain down then drew himself up from his lowly place, safe and sound, free to spring again from rock to rock, and eat the sweet grass on the hills.

Two other goats had left the valley, and climbed far up the mountain. At length they met on the banks of a wild, rushing stream.

A tree had fallen across the stream, and formed a bridge from the one side to the other. The goats looked at each other, and each wished to pass over first.

They stood for a moment with one foot on the tree, each thinking that the other would draw back. But neither of them would give way, and they met at last on the middle of the narrow bridge!

They then began to push and fight with their horns, till at last their feet slipped, and both the goats fell into the swift flowing stream, and were lost in the waters!

Both might have been saved, if either of them had known how to give way at the right time.

The New Royal Readers, Book II, *c.* 1885.

Father's Coming!

Father's coming down the lane,
I will run to meet him;
You come too, dear sister Jane,
Let us both go greet him.

He has been at work all day,
And he must feel weary;
I am sure that in the mill
It is very dreary.

Do you know, my sister dear,
I have just been thinking,
What we all should have to do
If father took t'drinking!

We should then be poorly drest,
Mother would be weeping;
We should have no soft warm
    clothes
T'cover us when sleeping.

But our father's very kind,
And he loves us truly;
We must love him in return,
And ne'er be unruly.

S. Knowles, *Every Band of Hope
Boy's Reciter*, c. 1880.

THE TRUTH-TELLER

A little boy had dropped a penny over a garden fence. When he found that he could not get it, he sat down and cried.

The owner of the garden asked the boy why he was crying.

'I have dropped a piece of money over the fence,' said he.

The man took a gold piece out of his pocket, and said to the boy, 'Is this the money you lost?'

'No, sir,' said the boy, who would not have told a lie for a great many pieces of gold; 'the money which I lost was not gold.'

'Was it this, then?' said the man, showing him a silver coin.

'No, sir,' said the boy; 'it was not silver.'

'Is this it?' said the man, showing him the penny he had lost.

'O yes!' said the lad; 'that is the *very* piece. I know it by the little hole in it.'

The man said, 'You are a truthful boy, so I will give you the gold coin and the silver one, and your own penny too.'

Every one loved the little boy, because he told the truth, and would not tell a lie to get money.

Another boy, who had seen the good little boy's money, and had heard him tell how he got it, thought he would try to get some money from the same kind man.

He ran to the garden and threw a penny over the fence, and then sat down and began to cry.

The man went up to him, and asked him why he was crying.

'I have lost some money,' said the bad boy.

'Is this the money you lost?' said the good man, showing him a gold piece.

'Yes, sir,' said the boy; 'that is the *very* coin!'

'Indeed it is not,' said the man; 'and for telling a lie you deserve to be soundly whipped. Be off.'

The bad boy thought he would gain by telling a falsehood; but the conduct of the good boy shows that it is always best to speak the truth.

Royal Readers; No. II, Third Series, 1879.

Friday

NEVER STEAL

You have now read of some of the naughty things which you are to avoid. There is another bad thing against which it will be well to caution you, and that is stealing or thieving.

This is a very bad and wicked thing indeed. There is not a little boy who has got a nice book or plaything, that would like to have it taken away without his leave by some naughty child.

He who does thus steal that which is not his own is never happy; he is always thinking he shall be found out, and that makes him afraid. And so though he has got what he wanted, he is not happy.

Neither is it right for a child to take anything which belongs to its parents without their leave. They will always give you what is good for you.

It is a silly thing for anyone to say, Well now, as no one sees me I will take it; for although no person may see you, yet the eye of the great God is on you: he sees you always, by night and day.

A little sweep knew this. He saw a gold watch in a lady's room. He was tempted to take it as no one was there. But God is here, said he. The lady heard him and was pleased, and took him and gave him new clothes, and sent him to school.

So he did better than if he had taken the watch, for then he would have been found out and sent to prison. Be honest; then God will bless what you do, and men will trust and honour you.

But if anyone begins to steal, he will perhaps go on to do so until he is found out, and then he will be called a thief, which is a foul name.

And if he begins to steal, he may go on until he gets into prison, and when he comes out, if he does so again, he will be sent over the sea a long way off for a long time.

> Guard my heart, O God of heaven,
> Lest I covet what's not mine;
> Lest I take a thing forbidden,
> Guard my heart and hands from sin.

The New Class Books for Sabbath Schools: Second Reading Lessons, *c.* 1875.

LESSON XXXV · ON THE CHOICE OF CLOTHING

1. The great object to be obtained by clothing in the variable temperature of this country is the preservation of the natural heat of the body. When a person feels chilly it is a sign that heat has been lost, or the proper action of the skin interfered with. All persons should be clothed so as not to feel habitually chilly. Whatever heat is lost by scanty clothing must be made up by extra food.

2. The entire body should be covered. The practice of wearing low-necked dresses is a bad one. It is very prejudicial to health to leave a warm room with the neck exposed; such a practice often results in violent colds, which end in consumption. Children require thicker, warmer clothing than adults: the common notion that children are made hardy by exposure to the cold is a false one.

3. In the variable climate of England, the practice of wearing flannel next the skin is good, especially for those persons who perspire freely. Calico is the next best to wear; it is cheaper than linen, and it is a worse conductor of heat. In winter the outer garments should be woollen.

4. The practice of compressing the waist by the tight lacing of stays is very injurious to health, and the younger the person the greater the danger, as the bones are much softer in youth than in adult life, and are therefore much easier injured. It should be borne in mind that the heart and lungs require a certain space in order to perform their proper functions. If this space is not given, disease must follow. The required space is not given when the waist is compressed. The use of stays should be dispensed with altogether: if children never wore them they would never want them. When worn they should not have steel ribs.

Another point to bear in mind respecting clothing is, that dress should really adorn, not disfigure, the person, and, therefore, though it may be necessary to dress in some measure according to the general fashion of the country, and the particular fashion of the time, yet we should not be slaves to fashion; and when any prevailing fashion is carried to an extreme we should be bold enough not to follow it. At the present day some of the modes of dressing the hair are anything but beautiful, and some of the hats and bonnets are decidedly ugly.

The Head-covering. – This should be such as will protect the head from the direct rays of the sun and the cold wind, and yet keep it cool. The brain is much easier injured by heat than cold; at the same time, whatever kind of head-covering is worn, it should afford protection to the eyes against the glare of the sun.

The Covering for the Feet should afford adequate protection against wet, cold and the irregularities of the ground; while the head should be kept cool, the feet, on the other hand, should be kept warm. Hence the practice of going out in the streets with very thin shoes is a dangerous one. Again, the shoes should not be pointed. When the feet are placed in narrow shoes the toes are pressed over each other, and this causes corns to grow, and renders walking difficult. If a shoe 'pinches' it ought not to be bought; and the notion that square-toed shoes do not look genteel should never be entertained.

Joseph Hassell, *Lessons on Domestic Economy for Elder Girls, c.* 1890.

THE MATERIALS USED AS CLOTHING

There is one more material, useful for maintaining heat in the body, that deserves special notice: that is *common paper.* It matters not whether it be white, brown, or even newspaper: *all paper* has a similar warmth-maintaining property to wool, and it has the further advantage of being cheap and light.

Our mothers and our grandmothers were right in using 'brown paper and vinegar', and in applying 'tallow plasters' to our chests and backs. They acted as well as our modern 'Allcock's Porous Plasters', and cost nothing.

To the poor the use of paper is invaluable as an addition to their clothing, so frequently thin and ragged. Ordinary newspapers tacked together, and strengthened by calico, however coarse, or a worn-out bed-quilt, will make warm and comfortable bed-clothes.

Brown paper sewn inside the waistcoat or back of the jacket will render a top-coat unnecessary, and a labouring man's wife can be as warm and cozy in a *quilted paper petticoat* as any duchess in her eider down and furs.

Wadding, in as thin a layer as you please, quilted between thick paper, will protect our chest and back through the coldest season. There is no need to spend our money on patent appliances, or expensive luxuries. We have used paper for some time as a substitute for linen and calico, in the production of ornamental clothing, as cuffs, collars, and shirt-fronts. Let us more fully recognize its true value as a warmth-maintaining material, easily obtained, and more easily employed than most woollen manufactures.

Joseph J. Pope, Simple Lessons for Home Use; Clothing, 1878.

THE POWER OF HABIT

I remember once riding from Buffalo to Niagara Falls. I said to a gentleman, 'What river is that, sir?'

'That,' he said, 'is Niagara River.'

'Well, it is a beautiful stream,' said I; 'bright and fair and glassy; how far off are the rapids?'

'Only a mile or two,' was the reply.

'Is it possible that only a mile from us we shall find the water in the turbulence which it must show near to the Falls?'

'You will find it so, sir.'

And so I found it; and the first sight of Niagara I shall never forget. Now, launch your bark on that Niagara River; it is bright, beautiful, smooth and glassy. There is a ripple at the bow; the silver wake you leave behind adds to the enjoyment. Down the stream you glide, oars, sails and helm in proper trim, and you set out on your pleasure excursion. Suddenly some one cries out from the bank, 'Young men, ahoy!'

'What is it?'

'The rapids are below you.'

'Ha! ha! we have heard of the rapids, but we are not such fools as to get there. If we go too fast, then we shall up with the helm and steer to the shore; we shall set the mast in the socket, hoist the sail, and speed to the land. Then on, boys; don't be alarmed – there is no danger.'

'Young men, ahoy there!'

'What is it?'

'The rapids are below you!'

'Ha! ha! we will laugh and quaff; all things delight us. What care we for the future! No man ever saw it. Sufficient for the day is the evil thereof. We will enjoy life while we may; will catch pleasure as it flies. This is enjoyment; time enough to steer out of danger when we are sailing swiftly with the current.'

'Young men, ahoy!'

'What is it?'

'Beware! Beware! The rapids are below you!'

Now you see the water foaming all around. See how fast you pass that point! Up with the helm! Now turn! Pull hard! quick, quick, quick! pull for your lives! pull till the blood starts from the nostrils, and the veins stand out like whipcords upon your brow! Set the mast in the socket! hoist the sail! – ah! it is too late!

Shrieking, cursing, howling, blaspheming, over they go. Thousands go over the rapids every year, through the power of habit, crying all the while, 'When I find out that it is injuring me I will give it up!'

Chambers's Elocution, 1898.

THE BEE

A little girl was once playing alone in a pretty garden. She was very young, and ran over the beds of flowers, and rolled on the grass, filling her little hands with daisies.

All at once the little child, as she was lying on the grass, heard a buzzing noise over her head, and looking up, she saw a large yellow and purple bee. The sun shone on its wings, and made them look as bright as gold; and she thought it was the most lovely insect she had ever seen. The bee whirled round and round her many times, as if at play; and each time it came nearer, she stretched out her little hand to catch it, but it was all in vain; and at length the bee flew far away.

The little girl then got on her feet as fast as she could, and ran after the bee, but it flew about above her reach, till it was weary, and at last settled to rest on a full-blown rose. When the child saw it remain quiet, she went very gently up to the rose-tree, treading softly on tiptoe; and when she came within reach, she suddenly stretched out her hand, and grasped both the bee and the rose at once.

The bee, angry at being thus treated, pierced through the skin of the poor little hand that held it. The wounded child screamed with pain; and the mother, hearing her cries, ran to her aid. She took the sting out of her hand, and bathed it with hartshorn. When the child was a little better of the pain and fright, her mother said to her, 'My dear child, do not seize hold of all you see that looks pretty, without knowing what it is you are going to touch. There are many pretty things that will hurt you.'

The Grade Lesson Book, First Standard, *c.* 1870.

HOW TO KEEP HOUSE ON SMALL INCOMES

Sydney Smith gave this valuable advice: '*When you are going to buy anything, first ask yourself whether you want it, then, whether you can do without it.*' If this advice were more generally acted on, a vast amount of money would be saved.

People who 'run tick', or have 'scores' are constantly tempted to buy what they don't want, or could do without, just because they haven't to pay for it at the moment, 'it can go down in the bill', and there is the comfortable feeling that the bill has not to be paid immediately; whereas, if the plan of paying ready money were kept to, the mere sight of the quickly emptying purse would go a long way in helping to restrain the desire for the tempting thing, and so the snow-ball of debt, which gathers so quickly, would never be begun.

Table showing how a labouring man with a wife and three children can live in the country on 15s. 6d. per week

	s.	d.
Rent	2	0
Bread and Flour	3	0
Meat and Dripping	2	0
Tea or Cocoa and Sugar	1	0
Butter and Cheese	1	0
Haricot Beans, Rice, Barley	0	6
Oatmeal for Porridge	0	6
Coal, Soap, Soda, Candles	2	0
Clothing	2	6
Club and Savings Bank	1	0
TOTAL	15	6

Vegetables and potatoes are to be provided for out of the garden. Extra work in harvest time, or the sale of fruit or early vegetables from the garden would provide money for the purchase of seeds, and with thrift and management the wife might do some washing, charring or needlework, to provide money to purchase a pig and some fowl.

The next Table is a different one. In this is mapped out the spending of £1 1s. a week by a young couple who have been brought up comfortably, and who could not live as agricultural labourers do.

Table of Expenditure of £1 1s. per week, on all the necessaries of life for two people

	£.	s.	d.
Rent per week	0	2	6
Food	0	10	6
Clothing	0	5	0
Coal, Wood	0	1	6
Soap, Oil, Matches	0	0	6
Club, Savings Bank	0	1	0
TOTAL	1	1	0

Table of Expenditure of 10s. 6d. per week on daily meals for two people

	s.	d.
Meat and Fish for daily dinners	3	2
Tea, ¼lb. at 1s. 4d., 4d.; ½lb. of Cocoa, 3d.	0	7
Milk, 1 tin of Swiss Milk	0	4½
Bread, 1 loaf per day, at 3d. per loaf	1	9
Flour, 5d; Potatoes, 6d.	0	11
Vegetables for week	0	4
Barley, Rice, Split Peas, Lentils, Haricots	0	6
Fruit for Puddings, as Currants, Sultanas, or Apples	0	4
Butter, 6d.; Cheese, 6d.; Suet, 4d.	1	4
Bacon, Eggs, or Fish for breakfast	0	9
Sugar and Milk for Pudding	0	3½
Condiments – Pepper, Salt, Ginger, etc.	0	2
TOTAL	10	6

The Sunlight Almanac for 1899.

LESSONS IN READING – FOUR LETTERS

Amy

Amy, Amy, run to the rill,
Take the jug, my girl, to fill;
Tie your cap and tuck your slip,
Fall not in, as in you dip.

Set you out! my love, 'tis late,
And I do not want to wait;
Tom and Will, and Jem and Joe,
Are to come to tea, you know.

I must stay at home to bake
For each rosy boy a cake;
'Tis not every day we see
Such a lot of lads to tea.

Fear you not! my Amy, too,
I will bake a cake for you;
So, my dear one, to the rill,
Off you set, the jug to fill.

Crusts in Soak for Chickens to Peck, or,
The Little One's Reading Book, by Pa, 1838.

A LESSON IN DRAWING

What We Plant

What do we plant when we plant the tree?
We plant the ship that will cross the sea.
We plant the mast to carry the sails,
We plant the plank to withstand the gales,
The keel, the keelson, the beam and knee;
We plant the ship when we plant the tree.

What do we plant when we plant the tree?
We plant the house for you and me.
We plant the rafters, the shingles, and floors,
We plant the studding, the lath, and doors,
The beams and siding, all parts that be;
We plant the house when we plant the tree.

What do we do when we plant the tree?
A thousand things that we daily see.
We plant the spire that out-towers the crag,
We plant the staff for our country's flag,
We plant the shade, from the hot sun free;
We plant all these when we plant the tree.

Tit-Bits Monster Recitation Book, c. 1900.

The Little Soldier

I am a little soldier,
And though but six years old,
Within my little breast there beats
A heart as true as gold.

I have no gun or bay'net,
Nor sword down by my side;
Nor yet have I a prancing horse
On which to battle ride.

I have no balls or powder,
And yet I'm proud to say,
The wicked foe I battle with,
Ere long I mean to slay.

The army I belong to,
Are all as brave as I,
And sooner than they'd conquered be
Will fight until they die.

Our Leader, General Temp'rance,
Oft cheers us as we go,
And tells us if but true to him,
We're sure to slay the foe.

Our enemy is stronger
Than some of you would think;
He has a dozen different names,
But his real name is drink.

He laughs to see such youngsters
March up and down so grand;
But never mind, he soon will find
How bravely we can stand.

Now won't you join our army?
Come, sign the pledge to-night;
We'll gladly put you through the drill,
And teach you how to fight!

S. Knowles, *Every Band of Hope Boy's Reciter*,
c. 1880.

Granny's Gone to Sleep

Granny's gone to sleep:
Softly, little boys;
Read your pretty books,
Don't make a noise,
Pussy's on the stool,
Quiet as a mouse;
Not a whisper runs
Through the whole house.
Hush! silence keep; Granny's gone to sleep.

Matthias Barr, *Hours of Sunshine*, *c.* 1880.

Two of Them

Grandfather's come to see baby to-day,
Dear little, queer little baby Ned;
With his toothless mouth, his double chin,
And never a hair on his shiny head,
He looks in the pretty eyes of blue,
Where the baby's soul is peeping through,
And cries, with many a loving kiss,
'Hallo! what little old man is this?'

Baby stares in grandfather's face,
Merry old, cheery old 'Grandfather Ned',
With his toothless mouth, his double chin,
And never a hair on his dear old head;
He scans him solemnly up and down,
From his double chin to his smooth, bald crown,
And says to himself as babies do,
'Hallo! can this be a baby, too?'

Little Recitations for Little Readers, selected by
R. C. H. Morison, 1898.

Going to Bed

Down upon my pillow warm
I now lay my little head,
And the rain, and wind, and storm,
Cannot come too nigh my bed.

Many little children poor
Have not anywhere to go,
And sad hardships they endure,
Such as I did never know.

Dear mamma, I'll thank you oft
For this comfortable bed,
And this pretty pillow soft,
Where I rest my weary head.

And I'll lift my heart in prayer
To the God that dwells above,
Thank Him for His watchful care,
And for all His tender love.

Little Poems for Little Readers, c. 1870.

SATURDAY

Good Morning

Good morning, good morning,
My little maid,
Where are you going to-day?
Good morning, good morning,
Kind sir, she said,
Over the hills and away.

Good morning, good morning,
Pray give me a kiss,
A kiss from that rosebud so red?
Good morning, good morning,
Said pert little Miss,
And that was all that she said.

Good morning, good morning,
Robin Red-breast,
Please will you sing me a song?
Good morning, good morning,
I'm building a nest,
And shall not have done all day long.

Mrs Charles Heaton, *Routledge's Album for
Children*, 1871.

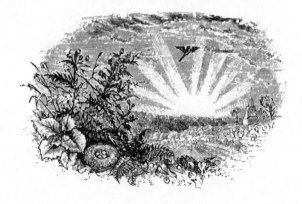

Sugar-Candy

A British boy loves cake and fruit,
A British girl the same, sir,
So bring them hither round about,
To have a little game, sir.
Pit and pat they all must go,
Pit and pat quite handy;
Then they next must roll the dough,
Thin, like sugar-candy!

A British boy loves holidays,
A British girl the same, sir,
And each will give a loud Hurrah,
Yes, even at the name, sir.
Let them get what I have here,
Choosing handy-spandy;
It is sweetness long drawn out,
For – 'tis sugar-candy!

A British boy loves dinner-time,
A British girl the same, sir,
And all will rush to take a place –
Except that they are lame, sir!
Never let their meat be sour,
Nor their pudding sandy,
Or they grumble for an hour –
Not like sugar-candy!

Jennet Humphreys, *Laugh and Learn*, 1890.

Guard Your Tongue

Guard your tongue from slander,
From the truth ne'er wander,
Wicked words be heard no more,
Draw a bar across the door.
Draw a bar across the door,
Wicked words be heard no more,
From the truth ne'er wander,
Guard your tongue from slander.

Guard your eye from error,
Look at sin with terror,
Poison oft may look like food,
Shun the bad, and keep the good.
Shun the bad, and keep the good,
Poison oft may look like food,
Look at sin with terror,
Guard your eye from error.

Guard your ear from list'ning
To the tell-tale's whisp'ring,
Wicked words pollute the mind,
Ne'er an entrance let them find.
Ne'er an entrance let them find,
Wicked words pollute the mind,
To the tell-tale's whisp'ring
Guard your ear from list'ning.

Learn your wits to bridle,
Let not one be idle,
Ear and tongue and eye may be,
Far too wild and far too free.
Far too wild and far too free
Ear and tongue may be,
Let not one be idle,
Learn your wits to bridle.

John Curwen (ed.), *Songs and Tunes for Education*, 1861.

[143]

BE NOT IDLE OR CARELESS

No one should be idle. When we are old enough to do something, we should be willing to learn how to do it, and then to do it as well as we can.

Even dumb creatures might teach us a lesson not to be idle. Birds and bees are busy, and work hard to build their nests, or gather honey all the day.

I once heard of a great big lad who laid himself down under a plum-tree, all the day long, with his mouth wide open, to let the plums drop into it; and his mother said he had nothing else to do.

And I have read of a woman who went about begging, and she had with her a big lad, and she said, My boy shall not work, for he may be a king some day.

Now were not both these women very much to blame, for bringing up these two big lazy lads in this way? They ought to have taught them to work for their own bread.

We must all work. We should not have any bread or clothes or houses if we did not work to get them; for God has said, By the sweat of your brow shall ye eat your bread.

The idle boy will turn out to be an idle man; and when his parents have done finding clothes for him, he will soon be covered with rags, without a house, or a fire, or a bed.

Learn, then, to do something; help your parents in anything you can do. Don't grumble when they send you on an errand, but make haste back. To loiter on an errand is naughty.

Get up early in the morning, then you will have rosy cheeks and good health:

> Early to bed, and early to rise,
> Will make us healthy, wealthy, and wise.

And always be neat and clean in your person; never be dirty. No one likes to see a dirty person. If you are clean and neat, you will both look better and feel better.

The New Class Books for Sabbath Schools: Second Reading Lessons, *c.* 1875.

TO THE IDLE

Lazy people ought to have a large looking glass hung up, where they are bound to see themselves in it; for sure, if their eyes are at all like mine, they would never bear to look at themselves long or often. The ugliest sight in the world is one of those thorough-bred loafers, who would scarcely hold up his basin if it were to rain porridge; and for certain would never hold up a bigger pot than he wanted filled for himself. Perhaps, if the shower should turn to beer, he might wake himself up a bit; but he would make up for it afterwards. This is the slothful man in the Proverbs, who 'hideth his hand in his bosom; it grieveth him to bring it again to his mouth'. I say that men the like of this ought to be served like the drones which the bees drive out of the hives. Every man ought to have patience and pity for poverty; but for laziness, a long whip; or a turn at the treadmill might be better. This would be healthy physic for all sluggards; but there is no chance of some of them getting their full dose of this medicine, for they were born with silver spoons in their mouths, and like spoons, they will scarce stir their own tea unless somebody lends them a hand. They are, as the old proverb says, 'as lazy as Ludham's dog, that leaned his head against the wall to bark', and, like lazy sheep, it is too much trouble for them to carry their own wool. If they could see themselves, it might by chance do them a world of good; but perhaps it would be too much trouble for them to open their eyes even if the glass were hung for them.

A man who wastes his time and his strength in sloth offers himself to be a target for the devil, who is a wonderfully good rifleman, and will riddle the idler with his shots: in other words, idle men tempt the devil to tempt them. He who plays when he should work, has an evil spirit to be his playmate; and he who neither works nor plays is a workshop for Satan. If the devil catch a man idle, he will set him to work, find him tools, and before long pay him wages. Is not this where the drunkenness comes from which fills our towns and villages with misery? Idleness is the key of beggary, and the root of all evil. Fellows have two stomachs for eating and drinking when they have no stomach for work. That little hole just under the nose swallows up in idle hours that money which should put clothes on the children's backs, and bread on the cottage table. We have God's word for it, that 'the drunkard and the glutton shall come to poverty'; and to show the connection between them, it is said in the same verse, 'and drowsiness shall clothe a man with rags'. I know it as well as I know that moss grows on old thatch, that drunken loose habits grow out of lazy hours. I like leisure when I can get it, but that's quite another thing; that's cheese and the other is chalk: idle folks never know what leisure means; they are always in a hurry and a mess, and by neglecting to work in the proper time, they always have a lot to do. Lolling about hour after hour, with nothing to do, is just making holes in the hedge to let the pigs through, and they will come through, and no mistake, and the rooting they will do nobody knows but those who have to look after the garden. The Lord Jesus tells us himself that when men slept the enemy sowed the tares; and that hits the nail on the head, for it is by the door of sluggishness that evil enters the heart more often, it seems to me, than by any other. Our old minister used to say, 'A sluggard is fine raw material for the devil; he can make anything he likes out of him, from a thief to a murderer.'

C. H. Spurgeon, John Ploughman's Talk, or, Plain Advice for Plain People, c. 1890.

I am a Little Weaver

I am a little weaver, and pleasant are my days,
My wheel is ever whirling, while round me kitty plays;
My life so calm and happy, so bright and active is,
There is no joy I wish for, to crown my earthly bliss.

My songs are never silent but in the peaceful night,
I always rise to labour when day is growing light;
But though I am so busy, I'm sure I do not care,
They rather should be pitied who always idle are.

I care not for the dainties, and all the splendid things,
That from beyond the ocean the rich man's money brings;
My daily food, so humble, I am content to eat,
Nor will I ever envy the wealthy or the great.

John Curwen (ed.), Songs and Tunes for Education, 1861.

LEARNING TO READ

'Why should I learn to read?' said Harry to his mother one evening as he sat with his book on his knee.

'For many reasons, which you will understand much better when you are older,' said his mother.

'But I do not like learning to read. I would rather work than read. Let me go errands and work in the garden instead,' said Harry.

'Let me tell you a story,' said his mother. 'A boy was once walking along a road, and at length he came to a bridge. On a post by the side of the bridge there was a board, with something written on it.

'The boy stopped when he saw the board, and read:

IT IS NOT SAFE FOR
PERSONS TO CROSS
OVER THIS BRIDGE.

'Thus warned, he turned back, and, taking another road, got to the end of his journey in safety.

'A little while afterwards another boy came to the bridge, who could not read. He saw the board, but he did not know what was written on it.

'So he went on; but when he got to the middle of the bridge, one of the planks broke, and he fell into the water, and was nearly drowned.'

Harry listened quietly till his mother had finished, and then he took up his book, and said, 'Thank you, mother; I think I had better learn to read.'

> If you would succeed
> In learning to read,
> Then say to your thoughts, 'Do not wander!'
> Fix well on your book
> Your heart and your look,
> That your lesson alone you may ponder.

One word will express
The way to success:
This word as a guide I will mention;
'Tis not very hard,
If you only regard
Its meaning: the word is – ATTENTION!

Royal Readers, No. II, Third Series, 1879.

LETTERS OF RECOMMENDATION

A gentleman once advertised for a boy to assist him in his office, and nearly fifty applied for the place. Out of the whole number he in a short time chose one, and sent all the rest away.

'I should like to know,' said a friend, 'on what ground you chose that boy. He had not a single recommendation with him.'

'You are mistaken,' said the gentleman; 'he had a great many:-

'He wiped his feet when he came in, and closed the door after him; showing that he was orderly and tidy.

'He gave up his seat instantly to that lame old man; showing that he was kind and thoughtful.

'He took off his cap when he came in, and answered my questions promptly and respectfully; showing that he was polite.

'He lifted up the book which I had purposely laid on the floor, and placed it on the table, while all the rest stepped over it, or shoved it aside; showing that he was careful.

'And he waited quietly for his turn, instead of pushing the others aside; showing that he was modest.

'When I talked with him, I noticed that his clothes were carefully brushed, his hair in nice order, and his teeth as white as milk. When he wrote his name, I observed that his finger-nails were clean, instead of being tipped with jet, like the handsome little fellow's in the blue jacket.

'Don't you call these things letters of recommendation? I do; and what I can tell about a boy by using my eyes for ten minutes, is worth more than all the fine letters he can bring me.'

Royal Readers, No. III, First Series, 1887.

I am a Cuckoo

'I am a cuckoo, my name is cuckoo,
The children call me cuckoo,
If you should ever forget my name,
I'll always tell you cuckoo;
When winter comes I hie away home,
In summer I live in the meadows.' –
So lives the cuckoo, his mate the cuckoo,
And all the little cuckoos.

Oh, hear the cuckoo, whose name is cuckoo,
And whom we all call cuckoo,
And who, though we should forget his name,
Will always tell us cuckoo;
When winter comes he hies away home,
In summer he sings in the meadows;
So lives the cuckoo, his mate the cuckoo,
And all the little cuckoos.

John Curwen (ed.), *Songs and Tunes for Education*, 1861.

Iron

Hid from our eyes, deep in the ground,
Great stores of gems and gold are found,
Rich mines of lead, and tin so fine;
But more than these, I prize the mine
Of rough, tough iron.

We make of gold bright seals and rings,
Fine chains, and other pretty things;
But spades and shovels, rakes and hoes,
Saws, axes, chisels, scythes, and ploughs,
Are rough, tough iron.

We make of silver, shining white,
Bright ornaments to please the sight;
But bolts and bars to guard at night,
And swords and guns our foes to fight,
Are rough, tough iron.

Then let me try to judge aright;
Oft useful things don't please the sight,
Things good for use oft are not fair –
I'll prize the things that useful are,
Like rough, tough iron.

The Royal Science Readers, Book I, 1896.

Song of the Engine-Driver

Oh – down by the river and close by the lake
We skim like the swallow and cut through the brake;
Over the mountain and round by the lea,
Through the black tunnel and down to the sea.
Clatter and bang by the wild riven shore,
We mingle our shriek with the ocean's roar.
We strain and we struggle, we rush and we fly –
We're a terrible pair, my steed and I.

Whistle and puff the whole day round,
Over the hills and underground.
Rattling fast and rattling free –
Oh! a life on the line is the life for me.

With our hearts a-blazing in every chink,
With coals for food and water to drink,
We plunge up the mountain and traverse the moor,
And startle the grouse in our daily tour.
We yell at the deer in their lonely glen,
We shoot past the village and circle the Ben,
We flash through the city on viaducts high,
As straight as an arrow, my steed and I.

Whistle and puff the whole day round,
Over the hills and underground.
Rattling fast and rattling free –
Oh! a life on the line is the life for me.

The Norseman of old, when quaffing his mead,
Delighted to boast of his 'ocean steed';
The British tar, in his foaming beer,
Drinks to his ship as his mistress dear.
The war-horse good is the trooper's theme –
But what are all these to the horse of steam?
Such a riotous, rollicking roadster is he –
Oh! the IRON HORSE is the steed for me!

Whistle and puff the whole day round,
Over the hills and underground.
Rattling fast and rattling free –
Oh! a life on the line is the life for me.

R. M. Ballantyne, *The Iron Horse, or Life on the Line*, 1871.

[152]

PROPRIETY OF SPEECH

1. You should be quite as anxious to *talk* with propriety as you are to think, work, sing, paint, or write according to the most correct rules.

2. Always select words calculated to convey an exact impression of your meaning.

3. Let your articulation be easy, clear, correct in accent, and suited in tone and emphasis to your discourse.

4. Avoid a muttering, mouthing, stuttering, droning, guttural, nasal, or lisping pronunciation.

5. Let your speech be neither too loud nor too low, but adjusted to the ear of your companion. Try to prevent the sad necessity of any person crying 'What – what?'

6. Avoid a loquacious propensity; you should never occupy more than your share of the time, or more than is agreeable to others.

7. Beware of such vulgar interpolations as 'You know,' 'You see,' 'I'll tell you wot.'

8. Learn when to use and when to omit the aspirate *h*. This is an indispensable mark of a good education.

9. Pay a strict regard to the rules of grammar even in private conversation. If you do not understand these rules, learn them, whatever be your age or station.

10. Though you should always speak pleasantly, do not mix your conversation with loud bursts of laughter.

11. Never indulge in uncommon words, or in Latin or French phrases, but choose the best understood terms to express your meaning.

12. Above all, let your conversation be intellectual, graceful, chaste, discreet, edifying, and profitable.

The Young Housekeeper as Daughter, Wife and Mother, compiled by the Editor of 'The Family Friend', c. 1870.

DEBT

When I was a very small boy, in pinafores, and went to a woman's school, it so happened that I wanted a stick of slate pencil, and had no money to buy it with. I was afraid of being scolded for losing my pencils so often, for I was a real careless little fellow, and so did not dare to ask at home; what then was John to do? There was a little shop in the place, where nuts, and tops, and cakes, and balls were sold by old Mrs. Dearson, and sometimes I had seen boys and girls get trusted by the old lady. I argued with myself that Christmas was coming, and that somebody or other would be sure to give me a penny then, and perhaps even a whole silver sixpence. I would, therefore, go into debt for a stick of slate pencil, and be sure to pay at Christmas. I did not feel easy about it, but still I screwed my courage up and went into the shop. One farthing was the amount, and as I had never owed anything before, and my credit was good, the pencil was handed over by the kind dame, and *I was in debt*. It did not please me much, and I felt as if I had done wrong, but I little knew how soon I should smart for it. How my father came to hear of this little stroke of business I never knew, but some little bird or other whistled it to him, and he was very soon down upon me in right earnest. God bless him for it; he was a sensible man, and none of your children spoilers; he did not intend to bring up his children to speculate, and play at what big rogues call financing, and therefore he knocked my getting into debt on the head at once, and no mistake. He gave me a very powerful lecture upon getting into debt, and how like it was to stealing, and upon the way in which people were ruined by it; and how a boy who would owe a farthing, might one day owe a hundred pounds, and get into prison, and bring his family into disgrace. It was a lecture, indeed; I think I can hear it now, and can feel my ears tingling at the recollection of it. Then I was marched off to the shop like a deserter marched into barracks, crying bitterly all down the street, and feeling dreadfully ashamed, because I thought everybody knew I was in debt. The farthing was paid amid many solemn warnings, and the poor debtor was set free, like a bird let out of a cage. How sweet it felt to be out of debt! How did my little heart vow and declare that nothing would ever tempt me into debt again! It was a fine lesson, and I have never forgotten it. If all boys were inoculated with the same doctrine when they were young, it would be as good as a fortune to them, and save them waggon-loads of trouble in after life. God bless my father, say I.

C. H. Spurgeon, *John Ploughman's Talk, or, Plain Advice for Plain People, c.* 1890.

The Spinning-Wheel

Nellie sits spinning the flaxen thread,
And thoughts come dancing into her head.
She thinks of Charlie far off at sea,
She thinks of what the future may be;
But the spinning-wheel ever sings the same song:
Hum hum hum, the thread is long.

Nellie thinks sadly of days gone by,
A tear-drop trembles in her blue eye;
But hope soon chases the tear away,
And Nellie's heart grows light and gay;
But the spinning-wheel ever sings the same song:
Hum hum hum, the thread is long.

Mrs Charles Heaton, *Routledge's Album for Children,* 1871.

SAM AND THE SLUGGARD

'Sam,' said a master to a sleepy-headed apprentice, 'have you ever seen a snail?' – 'Yes, sir.' – 'Then you must have met it; you could never have overtaken it!'

I want to tell such a lad his fortune; and I shall show it to him in two pictures, in the hope that he will mend his ways.

My first picture I shall call Mr. Sluggard's Plough. There, that is it, right in the middle of the field! He had been ploughing, you see, when it struck him that it was time to leave off; and that is the only thing he is ever in a hurry about.

Now, look at the work he has done. It is certain that Mr. Sluggard could not win a prize at a ploughing-match. How crooked the furrows are!

Sluggards did not take pains when they were boys. The man who is too lazy to plough straight, used to skip all the big words and the hard sums when he was a boy at school.

When I see a boy looking over his arithmetic book, and picking out the easy sums, instead of taking them as they come, I think I see Mr. Sluggard's plough.

The second picture I shall call Mr. Sluggard's Reason. For he *has* a reason why he is not ploughing today. His neighbours are busy. You may see them at work over the hedge, while the crows follow them, eating the worms that would otherwise eat the wheat.

Where is Mr. Sluggard? Yonder is his plough. Let us go and ask him why he is not at work. He lives in the village close by.

Let us ask this woman. – 'Do you know where Mr. Sluggard lives?' – 'Yes; that is the house: you may know it by the broken gate.'

Yes, this must be the house; the gate swings on one hinge only. Oh, what weeds in the garden! And you may see that the walls which were once white are now dirty yellow.

Knock at the door. No answer. 'He's not up yet,' says a neighbour. We wait till he gets up.

'Now, Mr. Sluggard,' we say, 'why are you not ploughing this morning?'

'Well,' says he with a yawn, 'it was very cold when I first awoke, and so I lay down again.'

Yes, that is the reason. There is no use for you to say, 'But was it not as cold for others, who have done half a day's work?' You will only vex yourself by talking with him.

The boy who does not like to learn because the lesson is hard, has Mr. Sluggard's reason. The girl who does not take pains to make her stitches small and neat, because to do so is 'a bother', has Mr. Sluggard's reason. And just as the cold does not hinder any one but Mr. Sluggard, so the difficulties that hinder some don't stop others.

'The cold!' Never mind the cold. Face it. Work all the harder because of it; and by so doing you will brace yourself for future toil, while your bed may only make you unfit for the duties of life.

Children! you may decide now what you will be in the future. If you are sluggards now, you will have no pity shown to you when you are older. If you don't work now, you may some day have to beg.

Royal Readers, No. III, Third Series, 1880.

THE SNAIL ON THE WALL

'What ails you, lad?' said Dame Bell to a little boy, who sat near a wall at the back of her house. He had a book in his hand, and tears were in his eyes.

'We have all got a poem called *Little Jim* to learn,' said the boy, whose name was Tom Blair; 'and the one who says it best is to get a prize from the master. But I don't think I can learn it.'

'Why not?' said the dame.

'The boys say I can't, and that I need not try,' said Tom in a sad tone.

'Don't mind what the boys say. Let them see that you can learn it,' said his friend.

'But I don't think I can,' said Tom; 'it is so long, and some of the words are so hard. I know I need not try for the prize. But I should like to learn the poem as well as I can; for the boys laugh at me, and call me "Slow Tom".'

'Well, dear,' said the dame, in a kind voice, 'if you are slow, and can't help it, try to be "slow and sure", as they say. Look at that snail on the wall; how slow it is! And yet, if you watch it, you will see it will get to the top in time. So just try to learn a few lines each day, and you may gain the prize in the end. And when you are like to lose heart, think of the snail on the wall.'

When Dame Bell had said this, she went on her way. And Tom thought that (though he could not keep up with the boys) he might run a race with the snail. So he resolved to try to learn his task, by the time the snail got to the top of the wall.

At last, the day came on which the master was to give the prize, and he called up the boys to repeat the poem.

When five or six had recited, it came to Tom's turn. There was a laugh when he got up; for most of the boys thought he would fail. But he did not miss a word; and his heart was full of joy when the master said, 'Well done, Tom Blair!'

When the rest of the class had tried, the master said that Tom had done best; and he gave him the prize.

'And now tell me,' said the master, 'how you learned the poem so well.'

'Please, sir, it was the snail on the wall that taught me how to do it,' said Tom.

There was a loud laugh when Tom said this. But the master said, 'You need not laugh, boys; for we may learn much from such things as snails. – How did the snail teach you, Tom?'

'Please, sir, I saw it crawl up the wall bit by bit. It did not stop, nor turn back, but went on, and on. And I thought I would do the same with my task. So I learned it bit by bit, and did not give up. And by the time the snail had got to the top of the wall, I had learned it all.'

'Well done, Tom!' said the master. – 'Now, boys, let us give a good cheer for Tom Blair and the snail on the wall.' And the old house rang with a loud, long cheer. For all were glad that 'Slow Tom' had got a prize at last.

Royal Readers, No. III, First Series, 1887.

The Young Abstainer

I am a staunch Abstainer,
Though very young you see;
And I intend, through all my life,
From drink to be quite free.

My father and my mother
Are Temp'rance people too;
My sisters and my brothers all,
Still to their pledge keep true.

Our little dog, named Friskey,
Turns up his nose at beer;
Our little puss makes quite a fuss
When drunken folk are near.

We have an old canary
Whose voice is very fine,
And he has never all his life
Drunk either beer or wine.

I wish every boy and girl
To-night could say with me;
My parents are Teetotalers,
And I will always be.

S. Knowles, *Every Band of Hope*
Boy's Reciter, c. 1880.

MY GRANDFATHER'S STORIES

LITTLE DICK AND THE GIANT

Poor little Dick; what a gay blithe fellow he was. He used to go singing and whistling about nearly all day: he was always merry, and scarcely any thing could make him sad.

One day, little Dick thought he would have a ramble in a large forest, at some distance from his home. He had often been to the sides of it before, but it looked so dark he was afraid to enter.

But Dick was more merry than usual on this day, for the sun shone so brightly, and the flowers looked so lovely, that he sang and whistled till he made the woods ring again. He delighted himself for some time among the trees and flowers; and, at last, seemed quite glad to have found out such a sweet spot.

There was a clear brook ran through the wood; and the waters looked so clean, that Dicky, being very thirsty, stooped down to drink; but, just at that moment, he was suddenly seized from behind, and found himself in the hands of a great, tall, fierce, ugly looking giant, a hundred times as big as himself; for Dick was not much bigger than the giant's thumb. The giant looked at him with savage delight; his mouth opened wide, and he made a noise which seemed to Dick quite terrible.

Dick thought the giant would have eaten him up alive, at one mouthful; he did not, however, do this, but took and put him into a large bag, and carried him off.

The poor little captive tried all he could to get out of the bag, but to no purpose, – the giant held him fast. He screamed, he struggled, he tried to tear a passage – the giant laughed, and carried him quite away.

At last the giant came to his house – a gloomy looking place, with a high wall all round it, and no trees or flowers. When he got in he shut the door, and took Dick out of the bag.

Dick now thought his time was come. When he looked round he saw a large fire, and before it hung four victims like himself, roasting for the giant's supper.

The giant, however, did not kill Dick; he took him by the body, and gave him such a squeeze as put him to great pain; he then threw him into a prison which he had prepared for him. It was quite dark, and iron bars were all round it, to prevent his getting out.

Dick beat his head against the iron bars; he dashed backwards and forwards in his dungeon, for he was almost driven mad. The giant gave him a piece of dry bread, and a drop of water, and left him.

The next day the giant came and looked, and found that Dick had eaten none of his bread; so he took him by the head, and crammed some of it down his throat, and seemed quite vexed to think he would not eat. Poor Dick was too much frightened to eat or drink.

He was left all alone in the dark another day, and a sad day it was; the poor creature thought of his own home, his companions, the sunlight, the trees, and the many nice things he used to get to eat; and then he screamed, and tried to get between the iron bars, and beat his poor head and limbs sore, in trying to get out.

The giant came again, and wanted Dick to sing, the same as he sung when he was at home, and to be happy and merry. 'Sing, sing, sing!' said he; but poor Dick was much too sad to sing – a prison is no place to sing songs in.

The giant now seemed quite in a rage, and took Dick out to make him sing, as he said. Dick gave a loud scream, a plunge, a struggle, and sank dead in the giant's hand. – Ah! my young reader, poor *Dick* was a *little bird*, and that *giant* was a *cruel little boy*.

William Martin, *The Holiday Book*, c. 1860,

Oh When's the Good Time Coming?

Oh when's the good time coming,
The good time promised long?
'Twill come when men are brothers,
Nor wish for what's another's,
And do no deed of wrong.

Oh when will War be over,
And nations live in peace?
'Twill be when pride and passion
Are gone quite out of fashion,
And spite and envy cease.

O God, forgive the sorrows
We to each other cause,
The cruel words oft spoken,
The wounded hearts nigh broken,
Our little private wars!

John Curwen (ed.), *Songs and Tunes for Education*, 1861.

THE HAPPY LAND

Mother. The country of which I speak, no foe can reach. That dearest blessing, freedom, for ever smiles upon its brave and honest tenants; while rolling seas and mighty navies form a firm and impenetrable barrier, to guard the sheltered land!

Helen. You are speaking of an island?

Mother. With a mild climate, never intensely cold, nor intensely hot; a fertile soil, which, with moderate labour, yields all the comforts, and most of the luxuries of life; laws open to the lowest as well as to the highest ranks of men, protecting the humble, curbing the great; a religion founded on the purest, simplest, and most benevolent doctrines; – what have these people to desire, but grateful hearts, to enjoy the blessings they possess?

Louisa. Quick, quick, mother, tell me where is this country; for I like the account of it better than that of any other I have ever heard or read of.

Mother. That the account is just, yourselves can bear me witness. For this land of which I speak – this fertile sheltered land of freedom – is ENGLAND! Because we live in it, we are apt to overlook its superiority, and imagine that other climes can yield higher joys. But this is a dangerous mistake; it makes us lose the pleasures within our grasp, in fanciful dreams of delight existing only in the imagination. Let us, my children, be wise! Let us acknowledge – let us feel – the real advantages our native land possesses! Let us be thankful that we were born in such a favoured country; and, pitying rather than envying the inhabitants of other climes, let us extend to them, whenever it is in our power, a share of our good things! If we travel, let us admire all that is beautiful in foreign countries, and respect all that is virtuous or wise in foreign nations; but never let us forget the high advantages of our dear native land! Let us do nothing to dishonour her present respected name! but let us firmly protect, and dearly love, our home – our favoured home – *Happy England!*

Key to Knowledge; or, Things in Common Use shortly and simply explained, by A Mother, 1841.

Saturday Night

The week is passing fast away,
The hours are almost done;
Before I rise, the Sabbath day
Will surely be begun.

Through all this week what have I done?
Have I been kind to all?
Have I sought any thing but fun,
And run at every call?

Have I been still when I was bid,
And ceased to make a noise?
Have I been good in all I did,
At lessons or at toys?

I'm naughty every day I live,
Say many a foolish word;
But God can pardon all my sins,
Through JESUS CHRIST, my LORD.

An infant's prayer He will not scorn;
I'll pray before I sleep,
And ask His love, then rest till morn,
For He my soul will keep.

Hymns and Rhymes for Children, c. 1875.

Saturday Night

Haste, put your playthings all away,
Tomorrow is the Sabbath day;
Come, bring to me your Noah's ark,
Put by your pretty music cart;
Because, my love, you must not play,
But holy keep the Sabbath day.

Bring me your German village, please,
With all its houses, gates, and trees;
Your waxen doll with eyes so blue,
And all her tea things, bright and new;
Because, you know, you must not play,
But love to keep the Sabbath day.

Now take your Sunday pictures down –
King David with his harp and crown,
Good little Samuel on his knees,
And many pleasant sights like these;
Because, you know, you must not play,
But learn of God upon his day.

There is your hymn-book – you shall learn
A verse, and some sweet kisses earn;
Your book of Bible stories, too,
Which dear mamma will read to you;
I think, that though you must not play,
We'll have a happy Sabbath day.

S. Prout Newcombe, *Pleasant Pages for Young People*,
1879.

SUNDAY

A Little Prayer

Father, when I kneel to Thee,
Hear the simple words I say;
Make a happy child of me,
Watch me, lest I go astray.
Make me true and kind and good,
Loved as little children should.

Matthias Barr, *Hours of Sunshine, c.* 1880.

Early Rising

Get up, little sister; the morning is bright,
And the birds are all singing to welcome the light:
The buds are all opening, the dew's on the flower;
If you shake but a branch, see, there falls quite a shower.

By the side of their mothers, look, under the trees
How the young lambs are skipping about as they please;
And by all those rings on the water, I know,
The fishes are merrily swimming below.

The bees, I daresay, have been long on the wing,
To get honey from every flower of spring;
For the bee never idles, but labours all day,
Thinking, wise little insect, work better than play.

The lark's gaily singing; it loves the bright sun,
And rejoices that now the gay spring has begun:
For the spring is so cheerful, I think 'twould be wrong
If we did not feel happy to hear the lark's song.

Get up; for when all things are merry and glad,
Good children should never be lazy or sad:
For God gives us daylight, dear sister, that we
May rejoice like the lark, and may work like the bee.

Chambers's Expressive Readers, Book II, 1892.

KEEP THE LORD'S-DAY

On the first day of the week we rest from all work, and are not to play at all. It is called the Lord's-day, for on that day the Lord Jesus rose from the dead.

And it is a good thing that we are to rest one day in seven: it is better both for us and the cattle. We are thus rested, and made able to begin our work again on the next day.

The poor heathen have no Bible, and so they have no Sabbath. To them all days are alike. They have no day of rest. You would not like that.

This is the day on which we are to worship and honour the great God who made us. We therefore go to the house of God to hear his word, and sing and pray, and hear the good news.

For on this day, the glorious gospel which tells us that Jesus Christ died for our sins, is made known to us, and happy and blessed shall we be if we love the Saviour Jesus Christ.

This day is always a happy time to those who fear God and love the Lord Jesus. A little girl was once asked if she loved to go to the house of God, and she said –

'I have been there and still would go,
'Tis like a little heaven below;
Not all my pleasure and my play
Shall tempt me to forget this day.'

Be you not like the dirty idle people who waste this day in sin and play: but early on the Lord's-day dress yourself neat and nice, and be found at Sabbath-school, and in the house of God, with them that keep the Sabbath holy.

And then if you love the Sabbath while you live, God will send for you to come up to him in heaven, to spend a long and happy Sabbath with him for ever with holy saints and angels.

And so mind and take care that no one ever persuades you to break the Sabbath, for that would offend the good and blessed God.

The New Class Books for Sabbath Schools: Second Reading Lessons, *c.* 1875.

Sunday in the Country

The spotted horse is put away,
The hoop, and kite, and top, and ball;
For 'tis the holy Sabbath day,
When Christians go to church and pray
To God, who loveth all.

To-day the doll is put aside,
The story-books placed out of sight;
For we must seek a holier guide,
And read how Christ the Saviour died
For us on Calvary's height.

The creaking waggon's in the shed,
The busy flail is heard no more;
The horse is littered down and fed,
The harness hangs above his head,
The whip behind the door.

His leathern gloves and hooked bill
To-day the woodman throws aside;
The blacksmith's fiery forge is still;
The wooden wheel of the old mill
Sleeps in the mill-dam wide.

The miller's boat is anchored where,
Far out, the water-lilies sleep;
You see their shadows mirrored there,
The broad white flowers reflected clear
Within the mill-pool deep.

The barrow's in the garden shed,
Hoe, rake, and spade are put away;
Unweeded stands the onion-bed,
The gardener from his work hath fled,
This holy Sabbath-day.

Upon the wall the white cat sleeps,
By which the churns and milk-pans lie;
A drowsy watch the house-dog keeps,
And scarcely from his dull eye peeps
Upon the passer-by.

And sweetly over hill and dale
The silvery-sounding church-bells ring;
Across the moor, and down the dale,
They come and go, and on the gale
Their Sabbath tidings fling.

From where the white-washed Sunday-school
Peeps out between the poplars dim,
Which ever throw their shadows cool
Far out upon the rushy pool,
You hear the Sabbath hymn.

From farm, and field, and grange grown grey,
From woodland walks and winding ways,
The old and young, the grave and gay,
Unto the old church come to pray,
And sing God's holy praise.

For the great God Himself did say,
Thou shalt rest one day in seven,
And set apart that holy day
To worship Me, and sing and pray,
If thou wouldst enter heaven.

Hymns and Rhymes for Children, c. 1875.

FAVOURITE HYMN COMPETITION:
AWARD OF PRIZES

The competition for your Ten Favourite Hymns was very largely taken up by our readers, no fewer than three hundred and eighty-eight boys and girls sending in lists, besides some twenty more, who, having omitted to send the coupons with their papers, were not admitted.

The following are the hymns which have been selected, with the number of votes given to each.

Votes	Beginning of Hymn
115	Rock of ages, cleft for me
99	There's a Friend for little children
93	There is a green hill far away
84	Jesu, Lover of my soul
81	Abide with me; fast falls the eventide
74	Onward, Christian soldiers
69	I heard the voice of Jesus say
66	Art thou weary, art thou languid
65	Lead kindly Light, amid the encircling gloom
62	Sun of my soul, Thou Saviour dear

Of the ten hymns that stand at the head of the list, and which we think most of our readers will agree deserve their position, three papers each contain seven, and the sender of each will receive Five Shillings. Their names are –

GEORGE KELLY (aged 12), New Cross;
SYDNEY M.O. HODGINS (aged 12), Liverpool;
FLORENCE GODFREY (aged 13), Penge.

* * *

We deeply regret to say that J. DALE, who received the First Prize in the Fable Competition last year, has been discovered to be quite unworthy of it, having copied her fable with a few alterations from one already printed.

It grieves us much that any of our boys and girls should be guilty of such dishonesty.

* * *

[ITEM IN THE FOLLOWING ISSUE OF THE MAGAZINE]

We are glad to be able to state that J. Dale has returned the prize which was wrongly awarded to her, explaining that it was through a misunderstanding, and not through any intention to deceive, that she reproduced Eliza Cook's fable.

The Boys' and Girls' Companion, 1894.

THE FARMER AND THE STORK

A Farmer sowed some seed in a field, and when it grew up and became grain the cranes ate it. The man feared that if he did not do something all his crop would be lost.

He set up a pole in the field, and on this pole he put an old coat and hat, and made it look like the figure of a man. When the cranes saw it they thought it was a man. They were afraid, and did not trouble the grain for some time. But at length they found out that this figure could not do them any harm, so they all came back again, and the field was in a worse state than before.

When the Farmer saw this he hit on another plan. He set a net in his field among the young grain and went and hid behind a tree to watch if any of the cranes were caught. In this way he took many of them and killed them.

One morning when he went out into the field he found that a Stork had been caught along with the cranes. The Stork was lame, and begged the Farmer to let him go, saying –

'Please, Farmer, do not kill me. I am not a crane. I am a Stork. I am a very good bird, and take care of my father and mother. Look at the colour of my coat, it is not the same as a crane's. Besides, I have not eaten any of your grain.'

But the Farmer said –

'I don't see how that can be. You say that you have not eaten any of my grain. That may be true, but you meant to do so, or you would not be here. I caught you with the cranes, and with the cranes you must die.'

'That's what comes of keeping bad company,' said the Stork, as the Farmer chopped off his head.

MORAL: If you are found in bad company you will receive the same punishment as your wicked companions.

My Book of Fables, c. 1895.

WISHING AND WORKING

'I wish the ground weren't so hard,' said an idle young sparrow to a robin, who was busily picking up some grains of corn that had fallen among a scattered heap of straw.

'So do I,' said the robin; 'but you see it generally is hard, this time of year.'

'Yes, I suppose so; well then, I wish there were more berries on the large hawthorn tree. It isn't worth while going to look for any even, for they are sure to be all gone.'

'Yes, you see it's a hard winter,' said the robin; 'and a good many

[175]

of your relations as well as mine have dined on it every day for this long while.'

'I know they have,' said the sparrow in a melancholy tone. 'Well, I wish I knew where to find some breakfast. I'm hungry enough; but I don't see any chance of getting any.'

'Nor do I,' said the robin, 'while you content yourself with wishing. If you set about looking for it, I think you'd stand a better chance. I've had a splendid meal while you've been "wishing" for one. Try my plan, and you'll find it will answer better.'

Eleanor B. Prosser, *Fables for You*, c. 1895.

Drive the Nail Aright

Drive the nail aright, boys;
Hit it on the head;
Strike with all your might, boys,
While the iron's red.

When you've work to do, boys,
Do it with a will;
They who reach the top, boys,
First must climb the hill.

Standing at the foot, boys,
Looking at the sky,
How can you get up, boys,
If you never try?

Though you stumble oft, boys,
Never be downcast;
Try, and try again, boys –
You will win at last.

Drive the nail aright, boys;
Hit it on the head;
Strike with all your might, boys,
While the iron's red.

Chambers's Expressive Readers, Book II, 1892.

[176]

OBEY YOUR PARENTS

Next to the fear and love of God who made you, it is your duty to honour and obey your father and mother. This is the command of the Lord in His own word; and it is very right.

Now just think of this. Don't be like those naughty or wicked children who do not care either for their parents or their God. They are going in a very bad way, and if they do not repent, will be ruined.

For who, when you were a little helpless baby, watched over you, and kept you from harm? Who fed you and clothed you, and was always ready to help you when you could not help yourself?

Did not your father and mother do all this, and more than this for you? Yes: and if they had died, then you would have soon found that neither uncle nor aunt would have done for you what they did.

Of old time, when the Jews were the people of God, if a son was stubborn and would not obey the voice of his father and mother, all the men of the city stoned him with stones till he died.

But the Lord was very good to those who loved their parents, as He said in the promise, 'Honour thy father and mother, that thy days may be long in the land which the Lord thy God giveth thee.'

Our Lord Jesus also, when he was a child, was subject unto his parents, and thus he grew 'in wisdom and stature, and in favour with God and man'. Try to be like Him.

If you thus love and honour your father and mother, you will grow up to be wise and happy.

The New Class Books for Sabbath Schools: Second Reading Lessons, *c.* 1875.

THE IDLE BOY

Why does that boy turn his face to the wall? He did not read well; he did not try to say his task like a good boy, and so he has been made to turn his face to the wall. Ask him if he does not feel sad. He says he does feel sad; he says too, he will be good, and that he will try to read well. May he come from the wall? Yes, Dick, you may come from the wall; and when you have read well, you may go and play with John and Ned; but do not cry, for I can not hear what you say when you cry. I dare say you feel sad, but it is of no use to cry. Wipe the tear from your eye, and try to be good, for if you are bad no one can love you, but we all love a good boy.

Mrs Barwell, *Little Lessons for Little Learners in Words of One Syllable*, *c.* 1870.

Weather Song

When the weather is wet,
We must not fret.
When the weather is cold,
We must not scold.
When the weather is warm,
We must not storm, –
But be thankful together,
Whatever the weather.

Longman's British Empire
Readers, Book 1, 1911.

TELLING MOTHER

A number of girls were standing talking together, when another girl joined them, and asked what they were speaking about.

'I am telling the girls a *secret*, Kate; and we will let you know, if you promise not to tell any one,' was the reply.

'I won't tell any one but my mother,' replied Kate. 'I tell her everything, for she is my best friend.'

'But you must not tell even your mother; you must tell no one in the world.'

'Well, then, I can't hear it; *for what I can't tell my mother is not fit for me to know.*'

I am sure that, if Kate continue to act in that way, she will become a good and useful woman.

As soon as boys and girls listen to words at school, or in the playground, which they would fear or blush to repeat to their mother, they are in the way of temptation, and no one can tell what may become of them.

Many a man has looked back with great sorrow to the time when first he allowed a sinful companion to come between him and his mother.

Boys and girls! if you would lead truthful lives, make Kate's reply your rule: 'What I cannot tell my mother is not fit for me to know;' for your mother is your *best friend.*

'Tis wrong for you to do a thing
That mother must not know;
And should your playmates, old or young,
E'er tell you so to do,
Leave them at once, and quickly go
To your dear mother's side,
Tell her – for well she knows what's wrong –
And she will be your guide.

Royal Readers, No. II, Third Series, 1879.

A Nursery Song

As I walk'd over the hills one day,
I listen'd, and heard a mother-sheep say,
'In all the green world there is nothing so sweet
As my little lammie with his nimble feet,
With his eye so bright,
And his wool so white:
Oh! he is my darling, my heart's delight.
The robin, he
That sings in the tree,
Dearly may dote on his darlings four;
But I love my one little lambkin more.'
And the mother-sheep and her little one
Side by side lay down in the sun,
As they went to sleep on the hill-side warm,
While my little lammie lies here on my arm.

I went to the kitchen, and what did I see
But the old grey cat with her kittens three.
I heard her whispering soft — said she,
'My kittens, with tails all so cunningly curl'd,
Are the prettiest things that can be in the world.
The bird on the tree,
And the old ewe, she
May love her babies exceedingly;
But I love my kittens there,
Under the rocking-chair.
I love my kittens with all my might,
I love them at morning, and noon, and night.
Which is the prettiest, I cannot tell, –
Which of the three, for the life of me, –
I love them all so well.
Now I'll take up my kitties, the kitties I love,
And we'll lie down together beneath the warm stove.
Let the kitties sleep under the stove so warm,
While my little darling lies here on my arm.

Sunday

I went to the yard and saw the old hen
Go clucking about with chickens ten.
She cluck'd and she scratch'd, and she bristled away;
And what do you think I heard the hen say?
I heard her say, 'The sun never did shine
On anything like to these chickens of mine.
You may hunt the full moon, and the stars, if you please,
But you will never find ten such chickens as these.
The cat loves her kitten, the ewe loves her lamb;
But they do not know what a proud mother I am;
Nor for lambs nor for kittens will I part with these,
Though the sheep and the cat should get down on their knees:
No, no! not though
The kittens could crow,
Or the lammie on two yellow legs could go.
My own dear darlings! my sweet little things!
Come, nestle now cosily under my wings.'
So the hen said,
And the chickens all sped
As fast as they could to their nice feather-bed;
And there let them sleep, in their feathers so warm,
While my little chick nestles here on my arm.

A Poetry Book for Schools, 1879.

REGARD YOUR TEACHERS

When you were a little baby you knew nothing. You are now learning to read. There are many things which you have to learn and know.

You often ask your parents about what you see or hear, and you are very pleased when they tell you something which you did not know before.

But parents cannot always be talking with you, as they must attend to their concerns; so they send you to school, that you may be taught to read and know many good things.

When your teacher is trying to instruct you it is your duty to mind what he says and try to learn; and you will soon learn if you mind your lesson well.

There are some children who are very careless, and do not mind their lessons, but are playing and talking in school-time. This is wrong, for children do not go to school to talk and play.

Regard what your teacher says. When you talk to a boy or girl, you do not like them to turn their backs and refuse to hear you. Then you must hear and regard your teacher.

There are many nice things in the Bible and other good books, and you will be so glad when you can read them. So lose no time, but learn as fast as you can.

In the Bible we read about how the world was made by the Word of God, who can make what He pleases. There we read about the first man and woman: how Satan tempted them to sin; and how pain, and sorrow and death came upon all men.

There we read about many good men, Abraham, Isaac, Jacob, Joseph, Moses, Samuel, David, and all the prophets, who told the people what God said.

And there we read how Jesus Christ came to save us from our sin, and how, if we believe in Him and love Him, we may be saved from death and hell.

The New Class Books for Sabbath Schools: Second Reading Lessons, *c.* 1875.

We Are but Little Children Weak

We are but little children weak,
Nor born in any high estate;
What can we do for Jesus' sake
Who is so high and good and great?

Oh! day by day each Christian child
Has much to do, without, within;
A death to die for Jesus' sake,
A weary war to wage with sin.

When deep within our swelling hearts
The thoughts of pride and anger rise,
When bitter words are on our tongues,
And tears of passion in our eyes;

Then we may stay the angry blow,
Then we may check the hasty word,
Give gentle answers back again,
And fight a battle for our Lord.

With smiles of peace and looks of love
Light in our dwellings we may make,
Bid kind good-humour brighten there,
And do all still for Jesus' sake.

There's not a child so small and weak
But has his little cross to take,
His little work of love and praise
That he may do for Jesus' sake.

Church Hymns, c. 1900.

The Happy Child

I thank the goodness and the grace
Which on my birth have smiled,
And made me in these Christian days
A happy English child.

I was not born, as thousands are,
Where God is never known,
And taught to pray a useless prayer
To blocks of wood and stone.

I was not born a little slave,
To labour in the sun,
And wish I were but in the grave,
And all my labour done.

I was not born without a home,
Or in some broken shed,
Like some poor children, taught to roam
And beg their daily bread.

My God, I thank Thee who has plann'd
A better lot for me,
And placed me in this happy land,
Where I may hear of Thee.

Hymns and Rhymes for Children, c. 1875.

The Best Use of a Penny

Should you wish to be told the best use of a penny,
I'll tell you a way that is better than any:
Not on apples, or cakes, or playthings to spend it,
But over the seas to the heathen to send it.
Come listen to me, and I'll tell, if you please,
Of some poor little children far over the seas.

Their skins are quite black, for our God made them thus;
But He made them with bodies and feelings like us:
A soul, too, that never will die, has been given,
And there's room for black children with Jesus in heaven.
But who will now tell of such good things as these
To the poor little children far over the seas?

Poor children in this land are well off indeed:
They have schools every day, where they sing, sew, and read,
Their church, too, on Sunday, and pastor to teach
How the true way to heaven through Jesus to reach.
Yet, sad to remember, there are few of these
For the poor little heathen far over the seas.

Poor blacks have few schools to learn reading and singing,
No Sunday for them with its cheerful bell-ringing;
And most little blacks have no Bibles to read.
Poor little black children, you're ill off indeed!
But one penny each week will procure some with ease
For the poor little heathen far over the seas.

Oh! think, then, of this when a penny is given,
'I can help a poor black on his way home to heaven.'
Then give it to Jesus, and He will approve
Nor scorn e'en a mite, if 'tis offered in love.
And oh! when in prayer you to Him bend your knees,
Remember your brethren far over the seas.

Hymns and Rhymes for Children, c. 1875.

CHOOSE GOOD COMPANIONS

Now, little reader, mind this, if you would avoid many of the bad things of which you have been reading, you will not choose a rude playfellow, for much depends on this.

For a rude boy will teach you bad ways. He will plague and tease you, and steal your playthings, and serve you many shabby tricks, such as you will not like at all.

A good boy would play quietly with you, and show you his nice books and playthings, and walk with you in the fields, and talk about what he has read, and help to learn you what is good.

We may thus know a good boy from a bad one. A bad boy will choose a rude lad for his friend, and a good child will choose a good one.

A bad boy will persuade you to keep away from school, and that is a very bad thing; for if you do not learn to read you will be a dunce, and know nothing.

A bad boy will ask you to run away on the Sabbath, and that is a very wicked thing. All who do so are in the way of ruin. Almost all mischief begins in breaking the Sabbath.

A good boy loves to go to school, that he may grow wise and good, and he will not run away on the Sabbath-day because he fears the great God, and loves to learn what is good.

It is better always to ask the advice of your parents about who should be your playfellows. They know better than you do. Be guided by them.

Behave well to your young friend. A friend loveth at all times. And if you love your young friend now, he may love you as long as he lives. Never forsake a good friend.

This is the way to live in love and peace here; and if we love the Lord, we shall go to the better world where all are good, and never do any harm at all. Angels and good people will then be our friends for ever.

The New Class Books for Sabbath Schools: Second Reading Lessons, *c.* 1875.

Jewels

When He cometh, when He cometh,
To make up His jewels,
All His jewels, precious jewels,
His loved and His own,
Like the stars of the morning,
His bright crown adorning,
They shall shine in their beauty,
Bright gems for His crown.

He will gather, He will gather
The gems for His kingdom;
All the pure ones, all the bright ones,
His loved and His own.
Like the stars of the morning,
His bright crown adorning,
They shall shine in their beauty,
Bright gems for His crown.

Little children, little children,
Who love their Redeemer,
Are the jewels, precious jewels,
His loved and His own,
Like the stars of the morning,
His bright crown adorning,
They shall shine in their beauty,
Bright gems for His crown.

Sacred Songs and Solos, compiled by
Ira D. Sankey, *c.* 1890.

PLAYING AND READING

It is very right that children should play. Play is a good thing for a little boy or girl. But then they must play at a right time and in a proper manner.

You must not play on the Lord's-day. That is wicked. For as the little hymn says,

> I must neither work nor play,
> Because it is the Sabbath day.

Neither must you play in school-time, either on the Lord's-day or on the week day. And if your parents tell you to do some other thing, you must not then run away to play.

When you play take care not to play with naughty children; and never play at what will harm you, or bring you into danger, or cause you to quarrel.

But beside learning to read and spell you must learn how to work. For as you grow up you will have to work as your father does now, to get bread and clothes and a house to live in.

The Romans always taught their children how to work, for they used to say, he who did not teach his child to earn his own bread brought him up to be a thief.

Little girls should learn to sew, and mend, and help their mothers; and little boys should help their fathers, and if they can, have a little garden of their own, and dig it and plant it.

The boy or girl who takes to these good ways is almost sure to grow up to be clever and useful, and will not want either food, or clothes, or house to live in.

And whatever you do, take care and do it well. There are only two ways of doing anything; and it is easiest and best to do all things well. It is sooner done, and looks better.

To do one thing well is better than to do many badly. So do one thing at once, and take care to do it well. Finish one thing well before you begin another.

The New Class Books for Sabbath Schools: Second Reading Lessons, *c.* 1875.

HYMN V

The glorious sun is set in the west; the night dews fall; and the air, which was sultry, becomes cool.

The flowers fold up their coloured leaves; they fold themselves up and hang their heads on the slender stalk.

The chickens are gathered under the wing of the hen, and are at rest; the hen herself is at rest also.

The little birds have ceased their warbling, they are asleep on the boughs, each one has his head behind his wing.

There is no murmur of bees around the hive, or among the honeyed woodbines; they have done their work, and lie close in their waxen cells.

The sheep rest upon their soft fleeces, and their loud bleating is no more heard amongst the hills.

There is no sound of a number of voices, or of children at play, or the trampling of busy feet, and of people hurrying to and fro.

The smith's hammer is not heard upon the anvil; nor the harsh saw of the carpenter.

All men are stretched on their quiet beds; and the child sleeps upon the breast of its mother.

Darkness is spread over the skies, and darkness is upon the ground; every eye is shut and every hand is still.

Who taketh care of all people when they are sunk in sleep; when they cannot defend themselves, nor see if danger approacheth?

There is an eye that never sleepeth; there is an eye that seeth in dark night as well as in the bright sunshine.

When there is no light of the sun, nor of the moon; when there is no lamp in the house, nor any little star twinkling through the thick clouds; that eye seeth everywhere, in all places, and watcheth continually over all the families of the earth.

The eye that sleepeth not is God's; His hand is always stretched out over us.

He made sleep to refresh us when we are weary: He made night that we might sleep in quiet.

As the mother moveth about the house with her finger on her

lips, and stilleth every little noise that her infant be not disturbed, – as she draweth the curtains around its bed, and shutteth out the light from its tender eyes, so God draweth the curtains of darkness around us; so He maketh all things to be hushed and still, that His large family may sleep in peace.

Labourers, spent with toil, and young children, and every little humming insect, sleep quietly, for God watcheth over you.

You may sleep, for He never sleeps; you may close your eyes in safety, for His eye is always open to protect you.

When the darkness is passed away, and the beams of the morning sun strike through your eyelids, begin the day with praising God, who hath taken care of you through the night.

Flowers, when you open again, spread your leaves, and smell sweet to His praise.

Birds, when you awake, warble your thanks amongst the green boughs; sing to Him before you sing to your mates.

Let His praise be in our hearts, when we lie down; let His praise be on our lips, when we awake.

Mrs Barbauld, Hymns in Prose for Children, 1864.

A Hymn of Prayer

Jesus, tender Shepherd, hear me,
Bless thy little lamb tonight;
Through the darkness be thou near me,
Keep me safe till morning light.

Through this day thy hand has led me,
And I thank thee for thy care;
Thou hast warm'd me – clothed and fed me,
Listen to my evening prayer.

Let my sins be all forgiven,
Bless the friends I love so well;
Take me, when I die, to Heaven,
Happy, there with thee to dwell.

John Curwen (ed.), The Child's Own Hymn Book,
c. 1865.

LIST OF SOURCES: ILLUSTRATIONS

The text and the illustrations are from books in the Rees-Williams Collection of Victorian Children's Books at St John's College, York.

For the text, the source is noted after each item. The illustrations come from:

COLOUR PLATES

The Child's Companion and Juvenile Instructor, 1891–1892
The Prize, February 1888, September 1889, October 1900
Through the Meadows, by Fred E. Weatherly. Illustrated by M. E. Edwards. *c.* 1895
Told by the Fireside, [stories] illustrated by Marie Seymour Lucas. *c.* 1890

BLACK AND WHITE HALF-TITLE PICTURES

MONDAY – *The Prize*, July 1888
TUESDAY – *Through the Meadows*, by Fred E. Weatherly. Illustrated by M. E. Edwards
WEDNESDAY – *The Prize*, January 1888
THURSDAY – *The Prize*, July 1889
FRIDAY – *The Prize*, December 1900
SATURDAY – *The Prize*, October 1890
SUNDAY – *The 'Original Poems' and others*, by Ann and Jane Taylor and Adelaide O'Keeffe, with illustrations by F. D. Bedford. *c.* 1900

BLACK AND WHITE ILLUSTRATIONS

At Home, illustrated by J. G. Sowerby. 1881
Babies' Classics, chosen by Lilia Scott MacDonald, illustrated by Arthur Hughes. Second edition, 1905
The Child's Own Magazine. New Series, 1881
The Golden Harp; Hymns, Rhymes, and Songs for the Young, adapted by H. W. Dulcken, PH. Dr., with fifty-two illustrations by J. D. Watson, T. Dalziel, and J. Wolf. 1864
The Illustrated Book of Songs for Children, edited by H. L. L., Author of 'Hymns from the Land of Luther'. *c.* 1890
Lullabies of Many Lands, Collected and Rendered into English Verse by Alma Strettell. With seventy-seven illustrations by Emily J. Harding. Second edition, 1896
Miller & Richards Typefounders Catalogue [For 1873]
Moral Songs, by Mrs C. F. Alexander. 1880
Nature Knowledge Readers (Rural Readers) Senior, by Vincent T. Murché, F.R.G.S. 1904

Old Friends in a New Dress. Our old Favourite Songs for the Nursery. c. 1890
The 'Original Poems' and others, by Ann and Jane Taylor and Adelaide O'Keeffe,
  with illustrations by F. D. Bedford. *c.* 1900
A Poetry Book for Schools. New Edition, 1859
Popular Temperance Recitations composed by Councillor Joseph Malins, G. C. T.
  October 1890
Royal Readers No. III, Third Series. 1880
Songs for the Nursery, edited by Robert Ellice. *c.* 1890
The Sunday Book of Poetry, selected and arranged by C. F. Alexander. 1864
The Works of Charles Lamb, Vol. VIII, edited by William MacDonald, with
  illustrations by Winifred Green. 1903

INDEX OF TITLES AND FIRST LINES

Titles are printed in italics

[194]

Index of Titles and First Lines